The Visionary Girls

The
Visionary Girls

WITCHCRAFT IN SALEM VILLAGE

MARION STARKEY

Little, Brown and Company · Boston / Toronto

Fifth Printing

T 04/73

Library of Congress Cataloging in Publication Data

Starkey, Marion Lena.
  The visionary girls.

  1. Witchcraft--Salem, Mass. I. Title.
BF1576.S83 1973   133.4'09744'5   72-13940
ISBN 0-316-81087-8

Published simultaneously in Canada
by Little, Brown & Company (Canada) Limited

PRINTED IN THE UNITED STATES OF AMERICA

For Ann Pantalone
Good neighbor and good friend

Author's Note

Tracing one's ancestry can be risky. What if one climbing the family tree finds an ancestor hanging from an upper branch in a literal sense, as the result of being condemned for a capital crime? Should the descendant conceal his discovery?

One famous group of condemned criminals, the men and women hanged in the Salem witchcraft, have multiple descendants. When my first book on the subject appeared, *The Devil in Massachusetts*, I heard from many of them. A letter from a descendant of Samuel Wardwell was particularly interesting. All his life he had been ashamed that an ancestor had been hanged for witchcraft. Reading my book, his shame was replaced by pride. For the first time he realized that his ancestor was heroic; he had renounced the false confession that would have saved his life and died defending the truth.

Wardwell's companions on the gallows were no felons, but victims of a delusion, and their descendants are proud of them. For more than a century the descendants of Rebecca Nurse gathered yearly at the Nurse homestead to honor their martyred ancestor. They do so no more, having become too many. But the beautiful homestead is still there, not in Salem, in Danvers.

The term "Salem witchcraft" is something of a misnomer; it might more accurately be called the "Danvers witchcraft," except that in 1692 no one had heard of Danvers. The place was called Salem Village, to distinguish it from Salem Town, five miles away. It was, however, in the present Danvers that the outbreak began and the first examinations held. Only in the later stages of the formal trials and the hangings did the scene shift to Salem proper.

In telling the story, distinguishing between the two Salems, village and town, presents difficulties. For instance, it is surprising that the excommunication of the much loved Rebecca Nurse was revoked many years later than that of the unpopular Martha Cory. The explanation is that Rebecca belonged to a different congregation, the First Church of Salem, meaning Salem Town, and its pastor, the Reverend Nicholas Noyes, did not share the zeal of the young Reverend Joseph Green of Salem Village for rehabilitating the unjustly condemned.

My first book was history in which I did not deviate from the records. Nor do I in this so far as characters and the general course of events are concerned, but I have made use of "poetic license" to enlarge on the records. So far as they go the latter are wonderfully rich in homely detail. We know that Mary Walcott brought her knitting to court with her, that Rebecca Nurse used a triple negative: "I never afflicted no child, no never in my life," that one magistrate forgot his grammar, saying "was you" instead of "were you."

But some records have been lost and they never contained the truth about what went on in the secret visits of the girls to the parsonage. Historians assume that they wanted Tituba to tell their fortunes, and that young Ann Putnam sought something like a spiritualistic seance. Fortune telling was a sin in the eyes of the Puritans; Cotton Mather denounced the practice as "little sorceries." The girls would have been severely punished had the nature of their errand been known. Ann Putnam's attempt to consult with the dead was more than a sin; it was a capital crime. The child knew it, and this knowledge, however carefully repressed, loaded her conscience with the guilt that underlay her hysteria.

I have invented the scenes with Tituba and the steps that led young Ann, many years later, to public confession, but they are what I believe really happened.

A few minor details. Why are some women called Goody, short for Goodwife, and others Mrs., short for mistress? It was a matter of social status. Mrs. was reserved for the gentry, like a minister's wife, or the sister of a magistrate, like Mrs. Isaac Porter. Goody was for humbler folk.

Also, why in court did magistrates use "thee" and "thou" and phrases like "who doth" though I present people talking otherwise in daily life? Because I think the dignified phrases were restricted to the solemnities of church and court, and I note that even in court the magistrates sometimes lapsed into plain "you."

The Visionary Girls

1

For six months in 1692 a pack of young girls, mostly teenagers, were all-powerful in Massachusetts.

These girls were very ordinary young people, some of them daughters of farmers in an obscure village, some of them servingmaids. A few had been taught by their parents to spell out their Bibles; others were illiterate. Yet ministers and magistrates who read Scripture in Greek and Hebrew and corresponded in Latin, hung on their words as if they were Holy Gospel. For a time the Great and General Court, as the Massachusetts legislature was called, conducted little business except that which concerned what came to be called "the visionary girls."

Perhaps the prophet Isaiah had the girls in mind when he wrote, "Every valley shall be exalted and every mountain and hill laid low." Girls of the period who had not yet achieved the dignity of marriage were of the valley, persons of no consequence, their opinions unsought, their cravings for attention suppressed. Now they were exalted, and the high were laid low. And what happened was the worst catastrophe in the Bay Colony since 1676, when the Indian chief King Philip united his followers in an attempt to drive the white men back into the sea which had brought them hither.

Indeed, it was a graver calamity. Not in numbers; only a score lost their lives as compared to the hundreds massacred by the Indians. But where communities at one time banded together against a visible enemy, they now fell into sore division when faced by an invasion from the invisible world. It was a long time, two and a half centuries in fact, before the Great and General Court effaced the last scars left by the Salem witchcraft.

The calamity arose not in Salem proper but in a settlement of scattered farms known as Salem Village (now called Danvers), a few miles inland. In 1692 the farm folk had for two decades enjoyed the right of organizing their own parish, building their own meetinghouse, and calling their own pastor. The arrangement had not gone smoothly. For some reason the village found it difficult to unite on its choice of pastor. Whatever majority carried the day, there was always a cantankerous minority determined to make trouble. Of the four ministers who had served Salem Village thus far, none had been happy. It was not surprising that the disaster of 1692 originated in the parsonage of the fourth.

He was the Reverend Samuel Parris, an able and energetic pastor. Unlike his predecessors, he had no degree from Harvard, but he had studied there long enough to read his Bible in Hebrew and to preach an

4

eloquent and closely reasoned sermon. None would ever deny his skill as preacher or his firmness in seizing and keeping the upper hand in his parish.

That he had no degree was due to no defect in his scholarship but to the fact that he had left Harvard to make his fortune in Barbados. That venture had prospered ill. Presently he recognized that it was not God's will that he lay up treasures on earth but in heaven, and guide the godly to do likewise. Returning to Massachusetts he looked about him for a pulpit. The only offer he got was from little Salem Village, and since he expected better, he let the farmers cool their heels for a year before he reluctantly accepted. Having heard of the troubles of his predecessors, he came determined to take no nonsense from anybody. He brought with him his wife Elizabeth, his little daughter Betty, his wife's niece Abigail Williams, and two slaves.

The latter represented the only visible fortune he had from Barbados. They were man and wife, John Indian and Tituba. The man did the heavy work about the parsonage stables and fields, and in slack seasons earned a few coppers for his master by serving guests at Ingersoll's ordinary, catercorner across the road.

Tituba's duties were in the house and, since the Parrises were often called out on parish affairs, included nearly full charge of the little girls. Her pet was eight-year-old Betty; a thorn in her flesh was Betty's cousin Abigail, three years older and impertinent. From Tituba Betty got more tenderness than from her own mother, whose expressions of affection were curbed by her husband's stern belief that a child was to be corrected not cuddled. Tituba's corrections were directed at Abigail and took the form of pinching and slapping.

"I'll tell!" shrieked Abigail on such occasions, but she did not. There was too much of her own misconduct that Tituba might have told. Besides, Tituba's tricks and tales were the chief entertainment of the children in the parsonage, and presently of the older village girls.

The first outsider to discover Tituba's qualities was sixteen-year-old Mary Walcott, whose home was close by. When a thanksgiving, one of the few jolly events in the Puritan calendar, was appointed just after harvest, Mary's mother had done a prodigious baking of pumpkin pies. Some were carried up to the cold loft for storage, some reserved for the family feast, and two of the finest were sent to the parsonage. They were removed from the cast-iron baking plates to wooden shingles, placed in a flat-bottomed Indian basket, and entrusted to Mary to deliver.

Mary had only to enter the kitchen to know that none of the elder Parrises were about. Their servants were idling. John Indian had seized the opportunity to lounge before the hearth in his master's own chair, and Tituba was snuggled with the children in the inglenook, Betty in her lap, Abigail at her feet. The children and John Indian were listening to a wonder tale she was spinning in her broken English.

At Mary's entrance the servants started up. Their master had no use for idling in broad daylight. When they saw it was only Mary, they settled back, and Tituba went on with her yarn. Mary found a stool, pulled out her knitting from the bag she always carried with her, and listened too.

At first she understood little. Tituba's syllables were blurred, her idiom peculiar to one not used to it, as were the Parris children. Mary was surprised when Betty suddenly gave a sharp cry of protest.

"Don't, Tituba, please don't. Don't tell about the duppy."

"You baby!" said her cousin. "The duppy's the best part. Tell it, Tituba."

"No!" wailed Betty, and clutched frantically at her nurse. Tears rolled down her cheeks and she looked on the verge of hysteria. "It gives me bad dreams. Please don't."

"Pay no mind to that baby," said Abigail scornfully, but Tituba cuddled the weeping child and shook her head.

"Tituba won't hurt Betty," she said. "Tituba love Betty." She looked at Mary. "I make you tea."

Mary sipped her tea from a mug and wondered. What was a duppy? Little as she had grasped of Tituba's tale, she had been impressed as Betty must have been by the tranced glare of the black woman's eyes as she spoke. She looked like a seeress with magical powers. After Betty's outburst Mary dared not ask about the duppy, but looking into her mug she had another idea.

"Tituba, can you read tea leaves? Can you tell my fortune in my cup?"

"That's a sin!" said Abigail at once. She loved Tituba's

talk of West Indian folklore, but her stern uncle knew about hell and what got you there. One way was telling a fortune by tea leaves. There had been a recent discovery of fortune-telling in the parish, and her uncle had preached a scorching sermon on the hellishness of tempting God's providence by the devil's devices. Betty at her side had wept, but Abigail had relished every word. The devil was as exciting in his way as the spirit Tituba called a duppy. But after that sermon she had no use for tea leaves.

Tituba had heard the sermon too. She shook her head. "Tea leaves not good. Leaves tell nothing, child play."

"Then you can't see the future?"

A faraway look came to Tituba's eyes. "When the spirit comes. When he comes and lifts veil, then Tituba sees."

Her eyes were hypnotic. Looking into them, Mary tingled with excitement.

"When they come, when the spirit comes, can you ask about me? Can you ask when I'll have a fellow?"

The children looked up at Tituba. Even Betty was quiet; to date her father had not preached against spirits who lifted veils. From his master's chair John Indian spoke up. "Spirit needs silver. Spirit not come without he sees shine of silver."

"Oh," said Mary. Silver was rare in Salem Village, where most people met their daily needs by barter. She personally had never owned so much as a six-pence. But Tituba had a kind heart. She grasped the disappointment behind that "oh." She knew very well how sixteen-year-olds crave to look ahead in anticipation of sweet-hearts. John Indian might say that such glimpses of the future could only be obtained through silver, but Tituba knew other things would suffice.

"Not silver only," she said. "Pretty things. The spirit loves pretty things. What you have he might like?"

Mary gave a downward glance at her neckerchief. It was a pretty thing, but if she gave it to the spirit there would be questions asked when she got home. She turned her mind to the odds and ends stored in her own little box, a sort of hope chest against the day when her fellow would come to claim her.

"Would the spirit like a ribbon, do you think? A red one? I have red ribbons at home and they're very pretty."

"You bring," said Tituba. "We see."

Her husband made a sudden leap from his master's chair and industriously poked at the fire. Tituba picked up Mary's basket and made a great show of arranging the pies on a shelf. Both had heard footsteps.

"Mama's coming," said Betty.

Her father came too. No one used such a homely term as "papa" in reference to the dignified Samuel Parris. He entered on a breath of cold air and threw a suspicious look at his servants. But they were both profitably employed.

"I fetch wood now," said John Indian agreeably, and departed. Mrs. Parris exclaimed over the pies.

"Why Tituba, they're beautiful! Did you have time to do all this while we were gone?"

"She," explained Tituba, pointing to Mary, who had risen from her stool in deference to the pastor and his gentle wife.

"They're from my mother, ma'am. We wanted you to have some of our thanksgiving baking."

"Bless her!" said Mrs. Parris. "I thank her from my heart. Will you stay and have a dish of tea with us?"

Mary was too shy to say she had already had one. Who knew but that it might make trouble for Tituba? Besides, she was anxious to get home, to ransack her chest for pretty things. She picked up her basket and her knitting and went into the gathering dusk. But instead of going home, she visited the Booth household and drew her friend Elizabeth aside.

"Spirits come to Tituba," she said, "and the spirits tell her what's to come. Only they need ribbons and things. Will you come with me?"

"When?" asked Elizabeth eagerly, and they conspired. They knew they must pick a time when neither the Reverend Mr. nor Mrs. Parris was about. Mary would also prefer a time when the children were absent, for she wanted to ask about that duppy. All this was difficult to arrange. It was more than a week before they heard that the Parrises were dining at Ingersoll's ordinary. They hurried to the parsonage, each with a bright ribbon tucked into her bodice. It was disappointing to find the children there, but it couldn't be helped.

What they learned amounted to little. Tituba's spirits gave her a glimpse of Mary's future husband, but since she had never seen him in the flesh, she couldn't name him. He was far away, in a forest. She saw Indians skulking among the trees. It looked as if he were on an expedition "to the eastward," that would be Maine, hunting down the red men. When would he come to Salem Village? Tituba didn't know.

"One day," she said. "You wait."

Elizabeth Booth learned that her fellow was somehow mixed up with shipping. Tituba could see masts behind him. She thought she knew this lad, but there was fog in the vision and she couldn't make out his features.

But if the girls got little information they did get hope. The dignity of marriage was not in the immediate future, but somewhere, in the wilderness, at sea, their true loves awaited them. Better than hope they got excitement. Both girls and both children felt an eerie tingling as Tituba stroked the bright ribbons and called to the spirit in an unknown tongue. They even felt the breath of the spirit as it came to lift the veil, and Tituba's tranced eyes, fixed on what she saw, all but hypnotized them. Little Betty was scared and whimpered, to be hushed by Abigail.

They crept away well before the parsonage folk could come from their dinner and find them here. They must do it again. Another time Tituba might see more clearly, and even if she could not, it was an experience not to be missed.

Winter was closing in, the dullest season of the year, and they would soon be housebound in a dreary round of spinning and churning and baking. Now that thanksgiving was over there were no feasts to break the

11

monotony. Christmas was just another workday in the Puritan calendar, its celebration considered a wicked Papist custom. If on that day a jolly red saint had descended on the village to distribute goodies from his pack, he would have been put in the stocks. Until spring released them to the gardens and fields, there was nothing to look forward to but Sabbath meeting—and secret meetings with Tituba.

They had left behind them two problems. When they had gone Tituba fixed sharp eyes on the children and said, "No tell." Abigail nodded, but Betty whimpered again. The seance had scared her, and now she knew there must have been something evil in it. Good children keep nothing from their parents. But she was devoted to Tituba and it was not in her to disobey.

The other problem was the "pretty things" the girls had brought. What to do with them? Tituba made a bow of Elizabeth Booth's blue ribbon and fastened it in Betty's golden hair. It looked lovely, but she dared not leave it. She would be asked how she had come by it. Before the parents could come she smoothed out the ribbon and tucked in into her bodice with the red one.

The problem remained. The ribbons might work loose and be seen. Even when she hid them in the straw of the pallet in the loft which she and her husband shared, she was still uneasy. She had no privacy even there, and if her master discovered them he would beat her as a thief. She almost wished the spirit had not asked for pretty things.

But John Indian, who had caused the problem with

12

his talk of silver, found a solution. Strangers passing through the village often stopped to sup at Ingersoll's, and sometimes gave him coins. No reason they couldn't also give him pretty things as well, like a bit of ribbon.

So little Betty wore a blue ribbon in her hair, and her cousin — who threatened to tell if she didn't get it — a red one in hers. But not for long. Parris deemed even the blue ribbon a mark of vanity, and the red one positively immoral. No child baptized a Christian could flaunt such a thing. He let Tituba wear it instead. A pagan might be allowed privileges denied a Christian, and Tituba was a pagan. She attended Sabbath meeting, bowed her head at family prayers, but remained an unregenerate heathen. The pastor had never thought her worth converting.

2

The events in the parsonage kitchen had been harmless enough. Tituba's consultants were merely young girls looking for a man, and what was wrong with that? If they had kept their secret to themselves neither they nor their village would have contributed a tragic page to history.

So far as their elders were concerned, they did keep it to themselves. Their excitement was not without a creeping sense of guilt. Reading tea leaves might be one thing and calling a spirit to unveil the future another, but stuffy grown folk would not appreciate the distinction. "What spirit?" they would ask, and indeed the girls sometimes asked each other.

But if they did not confide in their parents, they were less discreet with their friends. They couldn't resist dropping hints, making mysteries. When Susanna Sheldon, a neighbor two years their senior, gave herself airs about her prospects with a seaman expected back from the West Indies, Elizabeth Booth put her in her place by claiming a sailor for herself. "Who?" demanded

14

Susanna, and Elizabeth only looked knowing. It couldn't be told yet; later, in good time. But Susanna wormed the secret out of her, and not being as sure of her seaman as she said she was, she too rummaged around the household for a pretty thing and watched her chance to visit Tituba.

During gossipy gatherings between Sabbath meetings, girls who lived at a distance heard of Tituba's powers. Among this group were two seventeen-year-old maidservants, Elizabeth Hubbard, who served in the home of her aunt and her aunt's husband, Dr. William Griggs, and Mercy Lewis, who worked for the family of Sergeant Thomas Putnam. The news about Tituba also came to the ears of two who had already passed their twentieth birthday without finding a man, Sarah Churchill, servant to the lame George Jacobs, and Mary Warren, attached to the Procter family.

By January, Tituba had had nearly enough of the lovelorn maids of Salem Village. She enjoyed her modest celebrity as mother confessor, but there were too many demands upon her. Not that the girls descended on her in a body. That would have attracted attention; but they kept close watch on the comings and goings at the parsonage, and when the coast was clear one or another was always there.

Tituba was in danger of being flooded with pretty things. There was a limit to what John Indian could claim as gifts from transients at the ordinary, especially as winter closed in and such guests became rare. Much as she craved the keepsakes the girls brought her, she finally told them that the spirit no longer required pretty things.

One day Mary Walcott ran sobbing to the parsonage. News had come of an Indian raid on York "to the eastward." Was her sweetheart safe? She didn't know where he was or who he was, but he had become as real to her as her own family.

In her impetuous invasion of the parsonage, she was unable to consult Tituba's spirit. Mrs. Parris was there. A kindly woman, quite unlike her stern husband, she did her best to comfort the weeping Mary. No one yet knew how bad the raid had been, she said, but her husband would be the first to hear and she would relay the news.

"What is your young man's name?" she asked, and Mary became speechless and blushed. Mrs. Parris drew a natural conclusion. "Haven't you told your mother about him?" Shamefaced Mary hung her head. "You should, dear child. Keep nothing from your mother."

Before Mary left she caught the eye of Tituba, who nodded. She would consult her spirit when she could. It was not comfort but it was something.

Tituba was worried about the children, who were nearly always present at the seances with the girls. Abigail was an enthusiastic accomplice, but she was a saucy piece and not to be trusted. One day she might start bragging about her familiarity with the spirit. Betty worried her even more. The child was sensitive and fearful; the visits of the older girls with their lusty talk, the necessity of keeping a secret from her parents, was bad for her. She wept often and at night cried out in her dreams.

One morning at prayers, when her father ordered her to say a psalm, the child uttered incoherent gibberish. At least it was gibberish to the startled parents, but Tituba recognized an approximation of the dialect in which she summoned the spirit. Would the pastor also recognize the phrases from his Barbadian days? Mr. Parris, however, had not moved in voodoo circles. He cuffed the poor little Betty and sent her away from the table without her breakfast.

Tituba had had a severe fright. She began to dread the sight of a village maiden at her door, though in the kindness of her heart she could refuse no one. But when Mary Warren paid her a second visit and made an unseemly request, she ordered her never to come back.

Somehow the Warren girl, who lived at a considerable distance, got through light snow to the village not on the Sabbath, when all the Procters came, but in midweek. Even more remarkably, she eluded the attention of the other girls, hanging about the outhouses until she was sure of privacy, and then came in alone. When Tituba heard her request she understood her caution.

The young woman had not heard of the ban on pretty things. She began by laying before Tituba a shoe buckle. It was the finest gift that had come her way, silver to the eye, though lovingly fingering it, she knew that it was not. Tituba turned it over, showed it to the children, who exclaimed with delight, then handed it back.

"Tituba no thief," she said, and Mary exploded.

17

"You think I stole it? My master gave it to me when he lost the mate. It's for the spirit. Call him quick before someone comes. I need help."

"What help?"

Mary drew a deep breath. "It's my mistress, Betty Procter. She's cross to everybody. She says she owes me a spite. We think she's starting another baby."

Tituba stared. What sort of request was this? If Betty Procter was pregnant let her send for a midwife. Mary explained.

"Ask the spirit to lift the veil. Now, Tituba. She may die in childbirth. I have to know. Now."

"You want her to die?" said Tituba. It was a statement not an inquiry.

"I want to *know!*"

Tituba's eyes narrowed. Betty Procter was John's third wife. His last had died in childbirth. No longer young, he was a fine upstanding man of heroic build. If this wife also died, manless Mary could hope to replace her. It was a bad thought, and though Tituba was no authority on the Ten Commandments, she was tempted to order Mary out of her kitchen with no more ado.

The simple way to get rid of her was to do what she asked. It crossed Tituba's mind to fake a seance. But she was an honest seeress; she believed as firmly as the girls in her powers and in the reality of the visions that the spirit caused to swim before her eyes. She could not mock that spirit. Besides the children were there and would recognize any deviation in her incantation.

18

"Can't you hurry!" demanded Mary.

Tituba glared at her, but bowed and began her mumbling. Presently she lifted her head and stared blankly into the fire. Never had such a vision come before. At a great distance she saw a hill. Dim figures were mounting it toward a gallows. She covered her eyes, unwilling to see more, but the picture burned itself through her lids. She saw a woman she did not know; it wasn't Elizabeth Procter. She saw four men mount to the scaffold, and one was Mary's master. The children and Mary looked at her in silence. Tituba's expression was frightening. At last she found her voice.

"She not hang," she said mechanically.

"*Hang!*" exclaimed Mary. "Who said anything about hanging?"

"Baby save her life." Tituba spoke out of a trance in a monotone. "Her husband hang, she no."

Mary felt a spasm of terror then of fury.

"You're making sport of me! You're lying!"

The naturalness of her voice roused Tituba from her trance. She looked Mary up and down.

"Bad woman," she said. "You have bad thought. You bring bad thing. You go."

Mary couldn't believe her ears. A black woman, a heathen slave, ordering her out of the parsonage where any Christian had a right to be. She would stay as long as she had a mind to. But suddenly she changed her mind. She was badly shaken. It wasn't just Tituba, the looks of her, the strange words, but the children. Both had turned their gaze into the fire as if they could see what Tituba had. Abigail looked in fascination; the face of little Betty was a frozen mask of horror, yet this child who wept so often did not cry out.

Mary left. "And don't come back!" cried Tituba hurling the buckle after her. Then she turned her anxious attention to the children. She brought Abigail to her senses with a sharp slap. "I saw it! I saw it!" cried the child.

Tituba slapped her again and bent over Betty. The child's silence frightened her. It was as if she were caught in a nightmare from which she could neither wake nor cry out. She had never raised her hand against her nurseling, the love of her life, but might a slap help? Before she could make up her mind there came another knock at the door.

"No come!" she cried. "Today no." She was in no mood for the village maidens. But Abigail had already opened the door, and what came through it was not one of the lovelorn but a mere child. It was little Ann Putnam, a year older than Abigail, but hardly larger than Betty, and like her blue eyed, golden haired, and innocent of any interest in fellows. She came at her mother's request and bore an acceptable gift, a jar of jam.

Tituba welcomed the child. Her spirit, having departed, did not warn her that this innocent was the most dangerous visitor that had yet come her way.

20

3

There were two Ann Putnams, this child and her mother, wife of that upstanding citizen, Sergeant Thomas Putnam. Their home was little more than a mile out of the village center, but since the trail led through deep woods, it seemed farther. In Ann's early childhood her father had never taken his family to Sabbath meeting without carrying his musket across the pommel, on the chance that Indians were lurking in the brush.

There was good reason for such a precaution. Not long before his marriage Thomas had joined the village contingent in the "hungry march" to hunt down King Philip in the Rhode Island swamps. The chief had been killed at last and his followers either slain or sold into West Indian slavery, but the havoc King Philip had caused was not easily forgotten: whole settlements laid waste and the settlers massacred. Far as Salem Village was from the battleground, it still had a blockhouse for refuge against attack.

Though such Indians as passed through the village

nowadays came only to sell their baskets, they were not, in local opinion, as harmless as they looked. All were by definition devil worshipers, and while housewives dickered for their baskets, they kept a sharp eye on the vendors. Peddling gave them a fine opportunity for scouting. The blockhouse remained, and Putnam regularly drilled the militia on the village green to hold it in readiness.

He no longer, however, carried his musket to Sabbath meeting, and his eldest daughter, who like all Putnams had learned to ride early and well, had no fear of riding alone on her father's mare down the forest trail to the parsonage. Even if she had, she would still have gone, for this was her mother's errand.

The two Anns were more like sisters than mother and daughter, and the child was in some ways the more mature. Almost from babyhood she had understood the tragedy that darkened her mother's life and had studied the duty of protecting her.

How often she had seen her mother hovering over a cradle of a sick child and sobbing, "Oh it's dying, it's dying. Oh God help me, they're taking this one too."

To the frantic mother any ailment of babyhood was certain to be fatal. Once when a minister had attempted to console her, she had flown out at him. "We must accept God's will," he had said.

"God's will! It be the devil's will that kills my baby, and my sister's babies and my sister!"

She spoke of the aunt and baby cousins whom her own children had never seen, since they had died before their mother's marriage and their birth. To the eldest daughter, however, they were a vivid presence. Again and again she had heard the story from her mother.

Her mother had come to the village from her native Salisbury when she was hardly older than her namesake, to accompany her sister, the bride of the pastor, the Reverend James Bayley. It had not been a happy removal. The parish had not been united on this choice of pastor, and members of the opposition haunted the parsonage, looking for an excuse to get rid of him. Did he conduct his family prayers with seemly regularity? How sound was he in doctrine; how judicious in his choice of wife? Was she a fit helpmeet and a proper mother for their children?

Fit she was not, physically at least. Almost constantly pregnant, she was perhaps too young to give birth to healthy babies, and certainly too young to cope with what seemed to her the malice of this spying. She lost one child after another, and presently her own life. At that point her husband left the community. It was not he but his successor who had risked counseling the elder Ann about God's will.

She too married young, at sixteen, to a kind and long-suffering husband, and unlike the Reverend Bayley highly respected by the whole community. Young as she was, she became what the country folk called a "good breeder." Less than two years after the birth of her own namesake, she achieved one for her husband, little Tommy, and then came Elizabeth and Ebenezer and Deliverance and Timothy. The cradle was never empty.

23

Any visitor to the Putnam household was greeted on the doorstep by a swarm of little towheads.

Why then was not the mother content, blessed as she was, multiply blessed? Perhaps the blessings were too many for her, and came too fast, exhausting her strength. Perhaps her sister's tragedy had made her incapable of believing her own good fortune. Bearing live babies did not guarantee their good health. Young Ann had been delicate from birth, and the others had their colics and coughs.

Finally her worst fears were realized. A baby four months old had died of croup, "in agonies," as the mother said, "fit to pierce the stoniest heart." Her namesake, eight at the time, had with her mother hung over the cradle watching helplessly while the child gasped out its life. With her mother she visited almost daily the family burying ground to lay there fresh flowers in season, and when the frosts came, wreaths of pine cones. Nor did it seem strange to the child that the dead baby took precedence over the living. Was it not thus in the Bible, the good shepherd who left the ninety and nine for the one lost sheep?

It was at this time that the two Anns made visits to other graves, those near the meetinghouse, where Mrs. Bayley and her babes were buried. On the Sabbath, between the services of morning and afternoon, while most of the parish sat about the grass in fine weather, or in Ingersoll's ordinary in foul, to eat their bread and cheese and catch up on local gossip, the two Anns knelt by the graves, and the child listened to her mother's prayer.

"Oh God, is it thy will that the wicked shall flourish forever like the green bay tree? Is it thy will that those whose spite slew my sister and her babes go undiscovered and unpunished? The spite lives still; it has killed my babe and threatens the others. Oh Lord, discover this guilt to us before we are all lost."

When mother and child rejoined the other church-goers, they remained a little apart from the congregation. Though only the child had heard the prayer, her mother's temperament was well known, a woman incapable of forgiving an injury, a woman to whom bygones were never bygones but part of the living present. Who were those who had once tormented her sister with what was not, properly considered, spying at all but a decent church watch, by which members of the congregation assured themselves that there were no lapses from godly conduct? So long after, the incidents were imperfectly remembered. Best keep a distance from the suspicious eyes and sharp tongue of this woman, and enjoy the outgoing conviviality of her husband.

Thomas, seeing tearstains on his wife's cheeks, started to her with open arms. Then he abruptly checked the gesture. Husbandly embraces were a desecration of the Lord's Day, forbidden by law. A child born on the Sabbath disgraced its parents, for such a birth was considered — quite erroneously — proof that it had also been conceived on the Sabbath. Almost better a base-born child than that.

No such ban was imposed on the affections of a daughter. The younger Ann felt a shudder go through her mother at the unwelcome approach of Goody Cory, and putting a protective arm about her, used it to guide her mother in another direction. She knew her mother's dislike of Martha Cory as a self-righteous meddler.

But then she saw that little Tommy was leading his next brother in a romp unsuitable to the day, and left her mother to take charge of her siblings.

The younger children had long been her charge, and this duty was a care, but also the chief joy of her life. At home in the great kitchen, which was the heart of the household, she loved to hang over the cradle of the latest born and sing lullabies. She was a past master at feeding and burping; more skilled than her mother at distinguishing the cry of ill temper from the wail of real pain. She gathered and steeped the herbs that would ease a baby through the trials of teething. She was a sure hand with swaddling and changing.

Much as she loved infants, her joy increased when they became toddlers. She taught them to keep their distance from the great hearth, where logs crackled on the firedogs, not to touch the pots and kettles hanging from the trammel over it. She showed them how to make odd figures in the white sand, carted in from the Salem beaches, with which the floor was strewn. She kept them from reaching up to the table to overset her mother's workbasket, piled high with mending and knitting.

On the same table lay the great family Bible, from which Sergeant Putnam read morning and evening as the basis of the devotions known as "family duties." This she taught them was sacred, and until they learned to read, never to be touched. When she caught a child climbing up to explore the Book with grubby fingers, she slapped. That was the limit of her correction; she never slapped for lesser crimes.

Her happiest duties came with warm weather, when she could take the children afield to share her tasks in barn and garden. They helped her scatter the chicken feed, rummaged with her in the sweet-scented hay to find the eggs. They watched solemnly while she demonstrated the mystery of milking.

In the garden she taught them how to tell weed from plant, and how to pull one and cherish the other. When weeding was done she taught them little games. In spring there was the golden carpet of dandelions, lovely to look at and great fun to play with. Split the stems and they made curls. Cut the stems in sections and they were beads to be strung on grasses. When the blooms went to seed, became "clocks," they had an important function. "Blow them," said Ann, "and you can tell if our mother wants you."

Later in the year there were other flower games. When the burdock formed its burrs they could be clustered together to make little prickly baskets. Milkweed pods made fairy cradles and could be cushioned with tiny pillows made of their own floss.

Angels were very real to the younger Ann. Her favorite Bible story was the one of Jacob resting his head on a stone while a troop of angels sent to guard him went up and down a spectral ladder. She and the young ones sometimes acted out the scene, flapping their arms like wings.

She taught the children to sit still at Sabbath meeting, and to continue their devotions in a hut they built together of brushwood in a thicket by the orchard. She called it their booth, a term she had from the Bible. In the booth the children said their prayers, struggled with the catechism, and sometimes Ann preached a short sermon.

The Bible was the center of Ann's fantasy. Both her parents were educated, and under her mother's instruction she had early learned to spell out her favorite Bible stories for herself. There were no illustrations, no engravings in the family Bible, but it needed none. Ann's mind was vividly furnished with images. What she heard was for her immediately translated into pictures as real, as lively as the world about her. Given paint and brush the gifted child might have become an artist, or a "limner" as country folk put it.

When she turned twelve, materials of a sort were provided for her to work with. The angels of her childhood were replaced by devils. It was not for nothing that Ann became the leader among what the Salem magistrates called "the visionary girls."

It was at that time that her mother fell back into her habit of despondent brooding. Was she ailing? Her health had never been strong. Was she, like Elizabeth Procter, in an early sickly stage of another pregnancy?

Despondency was not, however, at that time peculiar to her. A wave of despair infected the colony at large; even hearty Thomas Putnam was not immune to it. The charter under which the Bay Colony had ruled itself since 1630 had been withdrawn some years ago. The eminent Boston minister Increase Mather had long been in England trying to negotiate a new one. Rumors flew about his difficulties. Some said that the very land titles given under the old one were no longer valid; that no farmer could claim his acres, cleared and tilled with back breaking labor. True or not, it was certain that the colonists could no longer elect their own governor; King William would appoint him. Nor could they keep the purity of what was most precious to them, their religion. The Church of England, from which they had fled to found their own Puritan worship, would be established on this holy ground, perhaps followed by the papacy itself.

Even the date was ominous. It was the last decade of the century. A conviction grew that the new one would bring the end of the world. The book of Revelation was urgently studied to learn the details of doomsday.

Revelation had long been Ann senior's favorite reading, but her despondency took a more personal turn. The dead haunted her dreams. She was beset with nightmares from which she woke up screaming. Her husband was tender, he was solicitous, but he was also a sound sleeper. It was little Ann who heard her first and scrambled up from her trundle bed to take her mother in her arms and caress her until the sobbing dwindled into shuddering.

No need to ask her mother's dream. It was always the same: little babies and their mothers in their winding-sheets calling to her to avenge foul murder. Young Ann entered into her mother's dream. The visions did not come to her in sleep; in broad daylight she clearly pictured the wailing babies. And she, like her mother, was often ailing.

Mercy Lewis their servant, a strapping seventeen-year-old who did the heavier work, one day came home from the village wide-eyed with an excited tale of Tituba's powers.

"She has a spirit, and when he comes he shows her the future."

The future had no interest for the elder Ann. "What of the past?" she asked. "Can she show that?"

Mercy Lewis didn't know. Antiquarian research was of no interest to her age group. When opportunity offered, the mother sent her namesake to find out.

4

It was some time before Tituba could give her attention to Ann's errand. She was too worried by the strange condition of her nursling.

Ann helped her with the child. No one knew better than she the occasional aftermath of a nightmare. Sometimes her mother passed from hysterical screaming to a speechless frozen immobility. The remedy was to take her in her arms, cuddle her, rock her, recall her to warmth and life by sheer love.

This remedy Ann applied to little Betty. Presently the child stirred, wept a little, and then fell into natural sleep. They tucked her into bed, and Tituba ordered Abigail to sit with her. The cousin objected. She wanted to see what fellow the spirit would bring Ann.

"No fellow this time," said Tituba. The newcomer's tender handling of Betty had won her heart. She returned to the kitchen ready to do whatever she was asked. "But not much time," she said. "Soon they come."

"Won't the spirit come if Reverend Parris is here?"

asked Ann. Mercy Lewis had barely hinted at the secrecy with which the girls conducted their seances.

"Don't tell Reverend. Don't tell anyone."

Ann felt her first qualm. Was there something wrong in this? Then she remembered what Mercy had said of her sweetheart. She had been after Tituba to tell fortunes, and that of course was wrong. Her mother's quest was different. She only asked an interpretation of her dreams; there could be no sin in that. Look at Holy Scripture: Joseph and Pharaoh; look at the prophets.

"This comes hard," said Tituba, and set to work. She knelt on the floor, drew a mystic circle in the sand, and began muttering. Presently she saw the babes in their winding-sheets.

"What else? What do the babies want?" whispered Ann. She also saw them, but not as Tituba did. For her they were revealed in the same way that she saw angels ascending and descending Jacob's ladder, through the light of her imagination.

"I see minister!"

"Is it the babies' father? Is it my Uncle Bayley?"

Tituba shook her head. The former Parson Bayley, no longer a reverend, for he had recently taken to the practice of medicine, came to Salem Village sometimes, and she knew him. This man she had never seen.

"He is black. He is black minister."

Ann had never heard of such a thing. She had never known a black to be received into church fellowship. How then could one enter the ministry? She could not picture this vision as she had that of the babes.

Tituba's gaze was still fixed on the invisible world.

"Woman now," she said. "Woman very old. She sits in grandmother chair."

That was all Ann learned that day. Tituba suddenly roused herself, studied the length of the shadows on the snow and said it was time to make supper. Her master was coming.

On her ride home Ann puzzled out the riddle of the black minister. Was he perhaps an Indian? Somewhere she had heard of a town of praying Indians for whom a minister had translated the whole Bible. Had one of these entered the ministry?

Her mother thought not. With her daughter she pondered Tituba's vision, and suddenly exclaimed, "She didn't mean black like her. She meant black hair, black eyes, dark skin. I know that man! Ann, next time ask if this minister is rather short."

"Next time?" The dutiful daughter would rather there were no next time. Now that she knew that her conference with Tituba was something that the pastor must not hear of, she felt guilty and afraid. She was still more afraid when one day her Uncle Joseph came in and caught some of the discussion of her mother's dreams.

Joseph came seldom to the Putnam household, where his presence was resented by his sister-in-law. He was her husband's half brother, child of the second marriage of the elder Thomas Putnam. When the latter died it transpired that he had willed the lion's share of his property to Joseph. The elder brothers sued, but lost the case since the property in question had come through the second wife. Since then the brothers were more or less reconciled, but their wives were not, particularly the elder Ann Putnam. Unfortunate that this man should happen upon her intimate discussion with her daughter.

"Ann, you brood too much on your losses," he said, startling them badly, for they had not heard him come. "You dwell on them by day, and so you dream of them at night. Can you never find it in your heart to accept God's will?"

The scene was almost what the child seemed to remember from her own infancy. The mother, caught off guard, was beside herself.

"God's will! *God*'s will? It be the devil that took my baby."

"Surely not without God's consent," said Uncle Joseph, sorry for her, wanting to comfort, but sticking to his point. Nothing, however, could appease the distraught woman.

"They come to me. My sister Bayley and her babies, my baby. They stretch out their hands, they try to speak. They try to tell me of the wickedness that killed them."

Joseph shook his head. "Ann, your sister's life was hard, and losing your baby was a sore trial. But the good Lord sends these trials to test the soul, and look how often he has blessed you. This girl," he tried to lay his hand on young Ann's shoulder, but she pulled away. "Your fine lads, and now this lady baby. Think of your blessings, Ann. Is it fair to the living to brood so much on the dead?"

"They come to me," said the mother hoarsely. "Night by night they call to me. They cannot rest while this great evil goes unavenged."

"Let me tell you a story," said her brother-in-law. "In Boston I met a trapper from the west, come to sell his skins. He told me of a woman in Springfield who grieved for her dead child as you do, and called to it until the devil brought it to her bed."

Both Anns were left speechless by Joseph's temerity. There was a brief silence broken by young Tommy.

"Then what happened?" he asked eagerly.

Uncle Joseph was somewhat vague on details. He wished he had questioned the trapper more closely. But one thing he knew.

"It was found out and became a hanging matter," he said. "But enough of that. Where will I find my brother?"

The child Ann was shaken to the depths by this tale. She tried to run at the false uncle who dared speak so to her mother, but her limbs stiffened in a queer paralysis, and when she tried to speak only choking sounds came out. It was some time before her mother and Mercy, working over her together, could bring her out of her fit.

It had somehow done her good. When she came to her senses Joseph had gone, and with him all memory of the terrible tale with which he had insulted her mother. At least it was gone from her consciousness. But below the daylight of her mind, in the dark place where dreams

35

are born, the memory remained, embedded in a cold sense of guilt and terror.

Whatever impression her mother had received from the fantastic tale had been wiped out by her fear for her daughter and her relief at her recovery. As the Sabbath approached she worked out a plan. The Parrises were often invited by good Deacon Ingersoll to enjoy the hospitality of the ordinary between services. That would leave the parsonage clear for her daughter to consult Tituba further about the identity of the black minister. Was he small as well as "black"? The elder Ann considered visiting Tituba herself, but that would involve a difficult explanation to make to her husband.

In the meetinghouse on Sunday, young Ann turned her attention to the gathering of the faithful to distract her mind from her dread of the coming interview. The day was overcast, the light came faintly through the windows, and there was cold comfort on the hard, backless benches. No heat was provided, though this was February; it would have been deemed an impiety. The pastor sometimes spoke with contempt of those women who brought little foot stoves with them to warm their feet. However he did not forbid it.

Ann set herself to counting the foot stoves. One had been placed under the feet of an old woman· whom she seldom saw here, for her affiliation was with the big church in Salem Town, and her sons and daughters brought her there to worship as often as they could. A matronly daughter supported her back with a strong arm for she was tremulous and feeble. She was also deaf, and when the first words came from the pulpit, Ann saw her strain forward and cup her ear to catch the word of God.

Who was she? It was an unlikely question in a village where everyone lived in everyone else's pocket, but Ann wasn't sure. She whispered an inquiry to Mercy Lewis.

"It's Goody Nurse."

Of course. This was Rebecca Nurse, wife of Francis, called the tray maker. Ann had heard much of the family from her mother, who considered that they were impiously trying to rise above the station to which God had called them. They were working together, Francis and his eight children, to buy the fertile acres that once had been part of the Endicott estate. They lived in the old Townsend-Bishop house, a house too fine for the likes of them.

Male and female sat on opposite sides of the church lest carnal thought distract the worshippers. The arrangement was not entirely successful. Some of Tituba's lovelorn maidens had managed to cluster together today, and Ann saw their eyes swing to the left where the fellows were. Mary Walcott could not take her eyes off a strange lad who might well be newly arrived from the eastward. Her benchmates Elizabeth and Susanna caught her at it, nudged each other, and then all three caught the giggles.

The service had not yet started; even so giggling was improper and was immediately reproved. Not by the tithingman, whose business it was, but by a stout matron whose business it was not. Martha Cory leaned forward and gave Elizabeth Booth a sharp rap. The girls fell resentfully silent. They hated Goody Cory, and out of her hearing mocked her pretensions to righteousness. "An old professor," she called herself, "a gospel woman."

Her husband Giles across the way was old as a man, but as a professor of the faith very young. He was a blundering, contentious man, often in trouble with the magistrates who had once held him to account for the mysterious death of a hired man. He had cleared himself of that charge, and recently, impelled by the incessant prayers of his Martha, had made his confession before the congregation and received the right hand of fellowship.

Beside him sat long, tall George Jacobs, who was no professor at all. He was very lame, got himself into meeting with the help of two canes, and did that seldom. Nearby sat a more faithful communicant, John Procter. He too swung his eyes to the opposite side, for he was concerned for the health of his wife. He caught not her eye, but the swooning gaze of his maidservant Mary Warren. Lately he had often caught that look from what he called his "jade," and it annoyed him. Sheep's eyes were very well for sheep, but not for this wench.

A subdued murmur came over the congregation. Mrs. Parris was coming down the aisle, the parsonage children at her side. After them strolled a yellow hound. It was not the dog that caused the murmur; one go-to-meeting dog or another was usually in attendance and no objection raised, provided he did not bark or commit a nuisance. It was the presence of the children that was unexpected. Word had got around that they were ill, strangely ill. No one knew the details beyond a report that Dr. Griggs had examined them and was baffled.

Yet here they were. Little Betty looked as if she might better have been left in bed. She stumbled along with downcast eyes, clinging to her mother's hand, and under her yellow hair her face was as white as the snowdrops just coming up in some gardens. Her cousin, however, had obviously recovered. Rosy and erect she walked confidently, her lively eyes searching out faces and costumes.

As they took their place forward, under the pulpit, Betty looked back and gave a little cry, promptly hushed by her mother. She was looking for her nurse Tituba, who was settling on a bench far back as befitted her humble station.

Then there was a clatter as people shoved back their benches and rose. The pastor was making his entrance and insisted on this mark of deference. It was not a universal custom, and here some resented it. But what the Reverend Samuel Parris commanded was in the end obeyed.

The watchful young Ann noted one exception. Rebecca Nurse's daughter Sarah made a move toward helping her mother to rise, then thought better of it. Alone of the congregation they remained seated while the minister in his black coat strode to the pulpit. Nothing that happened in meeting escaped this pastor; he also marked the defection.

The pulpit stood on a little platform, but hardly deserved its name. The meager rates of Salem Village had not yet been stretched far enough to provide a real pulpit, let alone a canopy over it as in the big churches in Salem and Boston. It was only a high table, but it had on it a proper cushion on which rested the great Bible. Today the pastor placed a slim volume beside the big one, and to the surprise of his congregation set beside it a lighted candle.

Why a candle? The light was dim indeed, but ministers got their sermons by heart. Today, however, Parris was making an innovation. He would devote the morning to reading his text, making some comments as he went; in the afternoon he would preach his sermon. The text was long and he did not trust his memory. It was none other than Michael Wigglesworth's *Day of Doom*.

A rustling went over the congregation. This stern pastor was not given to novelties, and to draw a text from anything but Holy Writ was a novelty. Many were well acquainted with the text, for the little book by a gentle Malden pastor had been a best seller in New England for thirty years. Some read it almost as frequently as their Bibles. They relished the jig time of the verses in ballad meter and shuddered at their import. But no one could deny that it was in these anxious times worth hearing, particularly in the dramatic utterance this pastor would bring to it.

He read slowly, deliberately, and at significant points paused to search out the eyes of his congregation.

> *Virgins unwise, who through disguise*
> *Amongst the best were number'd . . .*

40

Why then did he look past Martha Cory to the bench that contained Mary Walcott, Susanna and Elizabeth? The three felt a spasm of fright, especially when other heads turned to see who sat there. But he made no comment; the reading went on.

The young Ann Putnam kept her eyes on the forward bench where Mrs. Parris sat with the two small girls. Docile Betty had been one to sit utterly still in meeting, even when her father's thunders sent the tears to rolling down her cheeks. It was Abigail who wriggled and turned about and had to be reproved. Today their situations were reversed. The cousin was quiet, hanging raptly on the words; it was little Betty who writhed in her place and once half rose as if seeking escape.

> Forthwith he cries, Ye Dead arise,
>   And unto Judgement come.
> No sooner said, but 'tis obey'd;
>   Sepulchers open'd are;
> Dead Bodies all rise at his call . . .

Ann saw a vision. Once in Salem Town she had attended a graveyard ceremony and had looked into a tomb where the solemn coffins lay. That had not frightened her. But as she walked away she came upon a freshly opened grave where there was no coffin. A child had been buried in its winding-sheet, the fabric had rotted away, and Ann looked directly on a skeleton enclosed in remnants of corruption. Until today she had managed to thrust the memory from her waking mind, but now she saw it again. Was it so that the dead rose to face judgment? Was it so with the babies that haunted her mother's dreams?

She felt again the choking fit that her Uncle Joseph's story had brought on her. No one noticed; everyone was looking at little Betty.

"No! No!" screamed the child and this time rose. Her mother pulled her back and sought out her husband's eyes. Mutely she was asking his leave to take their child home. But he shook his head. Any earthly agony was better than the eternal torment that awaited the unredeemed.

He had practiced this reading in the parsonage in the presence of the children. Some verses had burned into his daughter's mind. Suddenly she silenced her father by shrilling a verse all out of turn:

> *The pious father had now much rather*
> *His graceless son should lie*
> *In Hell with Devils, for all his sins*
> *Burning eternally. . . .*

Then the child went into a convulsion. This time the mother asked no leave. She gathered Betty into her arms and carried her out. Tituba rose from her rear bench to help her, and the astounded communicants saw the child tear herself from her mother and clutch at the black woman.

There was no settling to an orderly meeting after that. Betty's collapse had sent a wave of something like hysteria over the congregation. Ann was helplessly choking. As if they had caught it from her, the girls near Martha

42

Cory began to gasp and gibber. John Procter looked anxiously to his wife. It was not good for her to be here. No one was unduly surprised even when Abigail went after her cousin and aunt, though she went on all fours, making hoarse sounds like the barking of a dog. Her performance roused the yellow hound from his Sabbath slumber. He followed, sniffing at her skirts.

Little Ann did not have to visit the parsonage after all, nor did she stay for the afternoon sermon. Her father brought her home and left her to the care of Mercy Lewis.

But two days later she had no choice but to carry out her mother's errand. She had recovered, and there was at the parsonage too good an opportunity to be missed. Mrs. Parris and the children had been taken to the home of good Dr. Griggs, so that he could study the strange illness. The Reverend Mr. Parris spent his daylight hours praying over them. Little Ann mounted the skittish young mare and rode through the forest to see Tituba. She hoped to have her to herself, but Elizabeth and Mary saw her approach and joined her in the kitchen.

Tituba also would have preferred that Ann come alone. She was lonely and worried and at loose ends. There was plenty of sweeping and dusting to occupy her, but she seldom did such things without direction. When the girls came she had just returned from a brief call at the ordinary to ask John Indian what news he had. Lonely or not, she frowned at so numerous an invasion.

"No fellow today," she told the older girls. "Spirit told you all he know."

"Mother wanted you to have these preserves," said Ann quietly, and placed them on the table. Tituba softened. This child might have been a sister to her Betty, whom she so missed. She reached out to stroke the silken floss of her hair.

Ann didn't know how to state her errand in front of the other girls. Her eyes said it for her. They looked up at Tituba with pleading and Tituba understood.

"Bad dreams still trouble your mother?"

Ann nodded. "Every night. And that black minister . . ."

"She *see* minister?"

Ann shook her head. "But she thinks she knows him. Can you see him again and tell how tall he is?"

Tituba knelt and began to sketch the circle in the sand on the floor. The girls knelt too. It was a solemn moment and seemed the thing to do. Elizabeth and Mary had never seen this rite; they held their breath.

It was Ann who first saw an apparition more terrifying than what Tituba was trying to summon: there at the inner door stood the Reverend Samuel Parris.

Tituba saw him next and her mouth fell open. Why wasn't he with Dr. Griggs praying for the afflicted children? She had no idea that during her visit to the ordinary he had returned and gone to his study. Here he suddenly stood with lowering brow, eyeing the scene in high displeasure.

The girls were paralyzed with shock. It was a scene

from the Day of Doom. Why didn't their pastor storm at them, curse them as infidels? It would have been easier to bear than what he did, which was nothing. Curtly he ordered Tituba to fetch a mug of cider from the keg, scowled at them again and disappeared. He would not forget what he had seen. Their doom was postponed and the more horrifying for its postponement.

Ann was shaken to those depths where lay the knowledge of danger for her mother. Terror caught her by the throat and cut off her breath. Tituba recognized the symptom and ordered Elizabeth to take her to her home. And in the Booth household all three girls fell to choking and writhing on the floor. No one could help them, not even Dr. Griggs when he was summoned. He could not see into hearts where lay the dread of immediate exposure of guilt — nor now could the girls themselves.

It was the pastor's discovery which had brought this on, and the pastor had discovered nothing. He had been working on his sermon, an enterprise that induced in him such fierce concentration that only an earthquake shaking his books from their shelves could have roused him. He had heard nothing from the kitchen, had been drawn there only by a sudden thirst. He had scowled at Tituba only because she was as usual trifling; the girls to him were so many shadows. He had gone back to his sermon and was preparing no doom beyond the usual one prepared for poor sinners.

5

The parsonage children were not long with the Griggs family. There were too many demands on the doctor for him to continue his observations at close range. Salem Village was in the grip of an epidemic. He was called out at all hours to attend maidens afflicted unto death. And while he dosed them with draughts and powders from his bag, straightened limbs contorted in convulsion, he pondered what manner of sickness was this.

It was as contagious as smallpox, one girl taking it from another. Susanna Sheldon, coming upon the three who had fled the parsonage, fell into fits herself. When Ann recovered enough to be brought home, she fell into convulsions as soon as she got there, and Mercy Lewis caught them from her. The elder Ann, worn out from caring for the pair of them, fought for control, and then collapsed. Thomas Putnam returned from a hunting trip to find his household in sore plight.

An outbreak of smallpox might have been easier to manage. The stricken could be isolated, appropriate medicaments administered, and presently the illness would run its course. This illness too ran its course, or at least it had remissions. Most girls came out of their fits looking none the worse, and remembered little of what they had suffered. But always their fits recurred.

The doctor went from house to house, followed by a troop of anxious neighbors, and made his examinations. It baffled him that girls in delirium showed no trace of fever. Certain symptoms, the rigidity of their limbs and the locking of their jaws, suggested epilepsy. But thumbing through his medical books he shook his head. Epilepsy this was not.

The Greeks had a word for such sickness, hysteria. The name derived from the Greek for womb and was based on the theory that this was a "female complaint." In that they were wrong. Males are not immune. Indeed, in the wider sense most of the Bay Colony was about to succumb to the hysteric mentality; those who preserved their sanity would do so at the risk and frequently the cost of their lives.

Faulty or not, the Greeks were closer to understanding hysteria than anyone for two centuries after the outbreak in Salem Village. But Dr. Griggs probably had no Greek; medical men then ranked little higher than mechanics and seldom had the solid classical education given the ministry. In any case he was unlikely to run across this hypothesis, which had been forgotten for millennia. When in the Middle Ages, especially after the devastation of the plague, much of Europe suffered outbreaks of mass hysteria, medieval doctors could only

47

ascribe them to the same cause Dr. Griggs finally did.

And what is hysteria, according to the theory evolved in the late 1800s after systematic study by psychologists? Are its symptoms a sham? "They do but dissemble," some villagers were to say of these afflicted girls. Not so; the ailment is real enough, and in its acute stages uncontrollable, though at the onset of the first seizure, the victim may have a degree of choice. It is not what is called insanity, for there remains some contact with reality. In mania a psychotic may do himself mortal injury; a hysteric does not. When he falls in a convulsion, there is something or someone to keep him from breaking his bones.

How does it start? The breeding ground is intense anxiety and emotional instability, a condition then prevalent in the Bay Colony. The girls who manifested it first were undergoing the stresses of adolescence, and all, even the child Betty, suffered a burden of secret guilt. In the morality of the time they had been involved in wrongdoing. The first seizure came, as is characteristic of these outbreaks, in a moment of near discovery.

Dr. Griggs made his diagnosis: "The evil hand is on them," he said, and all Salem Village shuddered to hear it.

Or most of the village. Martha Cory did not; she had no patience with these wayward females. Neither did John Procter. When his "jade" Mary Warren began howling the rafters down, he found a treatment which worked and recommended it to whoever would listen. He cuffed the girl smartly and plunked her down at the spinning wheel with orders not to stir from it until her work was done. Mary worked in tears, but work she did.

The doctor's diagnosis did not surprise the minister. It was what he had long suspected. He had been living in Boston three years earlier when a similar affliction had come upon the children of the God-fearing Goodwin family. The children, carefully bred and catechized, had suddenly become uncontrollable at family prayers, screaming out at the sound of the word of God and hurling the Bible from them. Betty, his own obedient little Betty, who knew every word of her catechism, had lately been doing just that.

In Boston the disorder had been traced to a witch named Glover, and only when she was hanged did the children begin to recover. Even then there were difficulties; in his study Parris had Cotton Mather's book describing his labors to rescue the oldest Goodwin child, Martha, from her bewitching.

These circumstances had preyed upon his mind, but until Dr. Griggs ruled out all other explanations he did not speak of them. Now his duty, the community's duty, was plain. The witches must be identified and brought to justice.

Everyone knew what a witch was. The lore derived from England, where in this troubled century witchcraft had become rampant. A witch was anyone, male or female, who bound his soul over to the devil in return for magical powers. These might include the ability to fly through the air, raise storms, cause epidemics, and what was relevant in this case, torment enemies at a distance.

Belief in witchcraft was universal in Massachusetts,

or nearly so. Martha Cory did not share it, and this would be a charge against her, for to deny the existence of witches is to deny the devil, which is the next thing to denying God. But if there was general agreement on the existence of witches, the means of identifying one was more in dispute. The subject was now ardently researched in old handbooks brought over from England. In the meantime the simple solution was to ask the girls.

"Who afflicts thee?" they were asked in the biblical language used on solemn occasions. "Dear child, who is it? Who afflicts thee?"

The girls were dumb. Their fits were as mysterious to them as to everyone else. They came and went as unaccountably as the wind. If Dr. Griggs couldn't explain them, how could they?

Some were beginning to enjoy their poor health. It often got them out of their more tedious household chores, it also brought them the most flattering attention. Until now they had been the obscurest members of the community, their opinions unasked, disregarded when offered. Now neighbors came in daily, even hourly, bringing custards and broths and infusions of herbs, and above all tender solicitude. "Who afflicts thee?" they were asked. "Dear child, who are these wicked ones?"

Strange, in view of their later conduct, that the girls had at first no answer. All had their grudges. Mary Warren detested her mistress Betty Procter, and most of the girls resented Martha Cory, who kept so sharp an eye on them in Sabbath meeting. But resentment was not enough and they did not cry out on these. Mary stood in too much awe of her master, and if they accused a good churchwoman like Martha, who would believe them? None had an inkling of the power about to be put in their hands, the day when their word would be accepted against the word of almost anyone in the colony. They were at this point only a pack of bewildered young people, falling into their fits and out of them without understanding.

Their worst attacks came when they were visited by their spiritual advisers. The Reverend Samuel Parris saw them daily, the Reverend Nicholas Noyes of Salem came often. Eventually all the ministers of the North Shore came in conclave for a day of fasting and prayer. Even more than the people of Salem Village were they appalled by what was going on. They were learned men; they had books in their studies, and from these they knew that the great witch plagues of Europe had begun, just as here, with innocent children. It was the devil's strategy against God's holy church to seduce the young and so undermine a whole generation. The souls of these young people were in terrible danger because the devil himself had commissioned his agents to snatch them from God. When the ministers prayed over the girls, their prayers contained something close to accusation. God had never permitted the innocent to be afflicted without opening their eyes to their tormentors. What concealment was there in the silence of these girls?

It was not surprising that the fits of the girls intensified during such prayers. In a way this was no new thing. Often in Sabbath meeting, when the sermon turned to the certainty of death, the damnation of the unregenerate, and an eternity spent tormented by the devil in the everlasting fires, they had broken down and cried out. But never as loudly as now when they were told on high authority that the devil had them in a stranglehold. They shrieked, they covered their ears, and some even hurled the Bible from them.

The ministers were not surprised. So it had often been in old England and on the continent; so it had been only three years ago in Boston when the Goodwin children were afflicted. Discover the witches, bring them to court, and the girls would be saved. To their prayers for the souls of these sufferers, they added a prayer that their eyes be opened, that the malefactors be identified whether their estate was high or low.

Meanwhile the villagers were looking about them to consider who among them were most likely to be dabbling in witchcraft, and found three. Warrants were sworn out on February 29 (for this was a leap year), signed by the good citizens Thomas and Edward Putnam, Joseph Hutchinson, and Thomas Preston.

No one could deny that those accused were plausible suspects, not even the skeptical Martha Cory. "If they are," she said, "I could not blame the devil for making witches of them, for they are idle, slothful persons and minded nothing that was good."

The trio were: a female tramp, a slave, and a matron who had got herself gossiped about. The matron was Sarah Osburne, who during the first years of her widowhood was said to be living in sin with her late husband's overseer. She had since married the man, but her sins were not forgiven her; moreover it was a year since she had shown herself at Sabbath meeting.

Few of the girls probably knew Goody Osburne, but everyone knew the other Sarah, Goody Good. She was the sort of vagrant whom New England villages "warned out," driving them from town, to get rid of a public charge. They could not so easily dispose of Sarah because she had a decent husband, William, who lived by hiring himself out to make hay or to harvest crops.

The Goods had no settled home. One child, Dorcas, had been placed with a Putnam kinsman. Another couple had once given the Goods refuge out of charity. They had put up with William, but Sarah was "so turbulent a spirit, spiteful and maliciously bent" that they had turned her out six months later. Sarah had retaliated by bewitching their cattle. They had what they deemed proof; when after losing seventeen head under mysterious circumstances they had charged her with the loss, she retorted that she didn't care if they all died. A woman who had refused to admit her to the house for fear of smallpox had also suffered loss.

Everyone had experienced the woman's begging at the door; if rebuffed she called the person vile names and went away muttering unintelligibly. A prudent householder would send to the barn to make sure the old woman didn't bed down in the haymow, for Sarah smoked a pipe and was careless with its coals. She also abstained from divine service. Why? she was asked. "For want of cloose!" she snapped, and indeed her tatters would have been unseemly in goodly company.

On March 1 two magistrates, Jonathan Corwin and John Hathorne, rode in from Salem to conduct not a trial but a preliminary hearing on the probable guilt of the accused. Thomas Putnam marshaled the militia to escort them to the meetinghouse, with banners flying and to the thrilling sound of fife and drum. All the village crowded in to watch.

Or nearly all. Martha Cory did not come and tried to keep old Giles out of harm's way by hiding his saddle. "But," as she said wryly, "he went for all that." John Procter objected to the order that he bring in Mary Warren, now quietly working at her spinning wheel. He was overruled; all the afflicted girls must be present so that the magistrates could judge how the proximity of the accused affected them. Reluctantly he obeyed and remarked, "She must have her fits forsooth."

That the magistrates expected conclusive results by confronting the accused with the girls was natural, indeed inevitable. How else were they to proceed? Adopting this course was, however, a grave mistake.

In their condition the girls were intensely suggestible. Already they were awed by the preparations for the examination, the beating of the drums, the prestige of the magistrates brought in from Salem. They had been told on august authority that their illness came from the devil through his agents the witches, and they had no reason for doubt. When a witch was brought before them, they faced her in terror. First one girl collapsed,

54

then another and another, the second catching the contagion from the first. None could see herself in her fits, and when recovered had no memory of them. But when she saw her companion infernally afflicted, her tongue protruding, her limbs contorted, and her eyes rolling back in her head, she felt the full force of the evil and fell into the same plight.

Very late in the day, in a rare moment of doubt, the magistrates were to undertake to question the girls singly and in private, and get a different result. Had that been their general practice, many innocent lives might have been spared, but this did not occur to them. The method they followed of assembling the girls in concert was that followed in old England and recommended in all their handbooks.

From the accused themselves the magistrates at first got little information. Goody Osburne, taken from her sickbed, quavered that she was "more like to be bewitched than be a witch." Goody Good, defiant before authority, had one reply to all charges, "I scorn it!" Though both were held for formal trial (Goody Osburne died before it could take place) their fate would have been an obscure episode in history but for the conduct of the third prisoner. She was Tituba, and Tituba "confessed."

Long after, when the hysteria that afflicted most of the colony had died down, Tituba reported how her confession had been obtained. Her master had whipped it out of her.

It had been a sore reproach to Parris that the abomination had begun in his own house. It was no longer a secret that the children in his care had been the first to be stricken. When the warrant was sworn against Tituba, his eyes were opened to many things to which he had given no thought before. How much she had been with little Betty, the first to sicken; how often she had sung to the child in her own barbaric tongue, incantations he now believed. At last he was aware that the other girls had often been with Tituba.

He beat the slave until he got a confession out of her. Not what actually had happened — no one was ever to report in rational terms what went on between Tituba and the girls — but in terms of the mad logic of witchcraft.

The silence of the afflicted girls on the origin of their torments was coming to an end. Little Ann Putnam had already broken it. The night before Tituba took the stand she had the first of a long series of nightmare visions. The witch came to her with a knife and tried to cut off her head. Ann's whole family was prepared to testify to this. Not that they could see her, for as is the way with witches, Tituba came not bodily, but sent her "shape," visible only to the victim; this was what came to be called "spectral evidence." But if the family saw nothing, they all heard the child's screams and watched her desperate struggles to beat off the witch.

How account for Ann's vision? She had always had the gift of what Wordsworth would call "the inward eye." In happier years of her childhood it had revealed angels to her, shining, winged creatures descending and ascending the ladder of Jacob's dream. She had that vision from Holy Writ, from the Bible itself. Now more ominous figures peopled her fantasies. Long ago she had shared her mother's recurrent nightmare and pictured the murdered babies in their winding-sheets. Once Tituba was accused by sober and God-fearing men as an instrument of the devil, Ann pictured demons as vividly she had once pictured the angels.

But now there was a fatal difference. Her illness was destroying her ability to distinguish between fantasy and reality. She was committed to a waking nightmare, and with it to a position of leadership among the afflicted girls.

Any doubts the magistrates might have had about Ann's vision when it was reported in court were stilled by Tituba's confession. Yes, she had gone to Ann's home to kill her and so prevent her from testifying. But not of her own will. Goody Good and Goody Osburne had forced her. And it was true that she had hurt Abigail and little Betty. It was done by pinching cats. She had at first refused. "I don't hurt Betty. I love Betty." But she was powerless against "a tall man from Boston" who threatened to thrust her into fire if she did not obey.

The man came to her in various shapes: "sometimes like a hog, sometimes like a great black dog." He was "something like a man" when "he tell me he was God and I must believe him and serve him six years. . . . I told him I not believe him God. I told him I ask my master and would have gone up but he stop me. The first time I believe him God he glad."

The man offered her presents, "some fine things, something like creatures, a little bird, something like green and white." One day he made her put her mark to a book he carried in his pocket, a book that contained other names. "Goody Good say she make her mark, but Goody Osburne no tell. She cross to me." There were meetings afield with the man. Transportation was apparently airborne, though Tituba was vague on details. "I was going and come back again. I never was at Boston. I never went to any town. I see no trees, no town."

The reactions of the girls were closely watched during these hearings in order to provide visible evidence of witchcraft at work. When the two Sarahs took the stand, one after another, the effect was obvious; the young people were pitiably afflicted. When Tituba was brought forward, their clamor was deafening. Then, strangely, it died down, and those who had been writhing and screeching a moment before, stilled to rapt attention. The reason was clear. In confessing, Tituba had renounced her witchcraft and tormented them no longer.

There was another circumstance that was not clear at all. The confession did not incriminate the girls. Not a word about the errands that had brought them to her kitchen: their unhallowed craving for fortune telling; Ann Putnam's desire to raise the dead. No one was ever to report these sessions, not even Ann, who alone of the girls was, many years later, publicly to repent her part in the prosecution of the witchcraft.

Toward the end of the hearing some of the girls began

to whimper again. "Who afflicts them now?" asked the magistrates.

Tituba shook her head. Having renounced her witchcraft she had lost her power to look into the invisible world. "I blind now. I cannot see."

On March 7 the three accused were bundled away to Boston jail to await trial, and the good people of Salem Village returned to their normal pursuits. For nearly two weeks the optimistic could hope that the incident was closed.

6

During the intermission several things happened of importance to the future. One that might have affected it for the better was an invitation from Cotton Mather. He wrote to the Salem magistrates offering to receive into his Boston home any six of the afflicted girls for observation and treatment.

He was already experienced in such afflictions as theirs. When the hanging of the witch Glover had not immediately cured the Goodwin children, he had taken the eldest, thirteen-year-old Martha, into his home, and kept her there until she was well.

Mrs. Mather must have shuddered at his latest invitation. She had been cruelly punished for not taking the antics of young Martha with proper seriousness. When the child's fits took the form of riding an unseen hobby horse up and down the stairs, she had been unable to smother a laugh. Shortly after, the devil appeared to her on her own porch, so frightening her that she gave premature birth to a deformed and short-lived baby. There was no laughter in Mrs. Mather after that, no matter what Martha did, and when her husband invited not one demon-possessed child but half-a-dozen into their home, it must have taken all her courage to face the ordeal.

She was spared, for the invitation was refused. One detail of Tituba's confession was much on the minds of the magistrates. From it they knew that the three arrests had not cleared the town of witches. The book to which Tituba had set her mark contained nine names. Who were the others? Tituba could not read, nor could she name two malefactors of whom she had caught an occasional glimpse, the "tall man from Boston" and a "woman in a white hood." They too must be discovered and brought to justice, and how could it be done without the aid of the girls, whose fits still recurred?

Rejecting the invitation was a pity. Cotton Mather was immensely popular with the young people in his congregation, and in his work with such hysterics as came his way, first Martha Goodwin and then two others, he achieved what a psychologist today would call a transference. Warming to his prayerful attentions, the girls fell more or less in love with him. All the afflicted of Salem Village, perhaps Ann Putnam and the two younger girls excepted, were ripe for love. What tragedy might have been spared the Procter family had Mary Warren been removed in time to the society of the personable young pastor.

But the magistrates needed the girls. They knew that Mather's therapy was prayer. That had been already administered in Salem Village by a conference of North

Shore ministers held on March 11. Those prayers did not restore the girls. How could they expect better of Mather's? — for all his eminence.

One girl was removed from the circle, however; little Betty Parris. Younger than the others, this child had suffered gravely. Whereas her cousin Abigail came out of her fits rosy and refreshed, Betty was sinking into severe illness. When Stephen Sewall of Salem offered to take her into his family, Parris hesitated, but his wife insisted that the child go. A soft-spoken, obedient wife, she was in this matter firm. She wanted her child removed from the hysterical clamor of the older girls, from the capers of her cousin, from the watchful curiosity of the neighbors. And it was done. Though at first Betty scared her hosts by her writhing and sobbing, little by little she grew well, became an ordinary little girl going about ordinary household duties.

The magistrates were banking on the ability of the other girls to see and name their tormentors. The first arrests had already opened their eyes to the invisible world. The night before the examination Ann Putnam had seen Tituba, and in court all the girls recognized the three accused as their tormentors.

Little Ann saw yet another. During the Good hearing she was bitten and saw the biter, Sarah's five-year-old daughter Dorcas. This she reported, but the magistrates took no action. Ann had not yet won her reputation as a "visionary maid," the one who could see farther and more clearly than any. Nor had the magistrates wholly yielded to the hysteria that was to overwhelm most of

Massachusetts. A five-year-old witch struck them as improbable.

That the girls soon began to name other witches had two causes. The popular theory was that their eyes were opened by use of a "witch cake." Mary Sibley, aunt of Mary Walcott, remembered this old world recipe and gave it a try. With the aid of John Indian she obtained urine from the parsonage children, mixed it with rye, baked it on the parsonage hearth, and fed it to the Parris dog. It was then and then only that the afflicted began to see their tormentors.

The pastor, as usual, had no idea of the indecent use made of his kitchen. When he was told he was exceedingly angry. He called the recipe "going to the devil to get help against the devil," and had Goody Sibley make open confession before a Sabbath meeting. Her sins were forgiven her. Many were privately grateful to her, since at last the girls were able to name the witches. Others were not, for the girls no longer named outcasts but people of good report.

"Hang them! They'll make witches of us all!" cried John Procter, speaking of the girls. "They should be at the whipping post."

Lame old George Jacobs looked on the antics of his servingmaid Sarah Churchill, listened to the accounts of her colleagues in affliction, and coined a rude phrase. "Bitch witches," he called the lot. These remarks, his and John Procter's, would not be forgiven them, but their time was not yet.

Whatever the merits of the witch cake, the more

probable cause of the girls' improved vision was that their friends had taken to asking them what a lawyer would call "leading questions." "Who afflicts thee?" had gotten no response. "Doth so and so afflict thee?" presently did.

Had Cotton Mather been present he might have warned the villagers against such a practice, as he had already warned his Boston congregation against irresponsible accusations. "An ill look or a cross word will make a witch with many people, who may on more ground be counted so themselves," he had said. "There has been a fearful deal of injury done in this way in this town to the good name of the most credible persons in it. Persons of more goodness and esteem than any of their calumnious abusers have been defamed for witches about this country — a country full of lies."

If such was true in sober Boston, how much more so in little Salem Village, which had been rent with contention ever since it became a separate parish, and where nearly everybody had at one time or another given a neighbor "an ill look or a cross word." In search of evidence many visitors worked upon the girls. Neighbors dropped in to make suggestions; aunts, uncles, parents drew one girl or another aside for a private consultation. And no one was more zealous in this endeavor than the elder Ann Putnam.

Such suggestions, it is true, were not accusations. To ask "Doth so and so afflict thee?" is not to accuse. But the effect on the girls was disastrous.

Hysteria has much in common with hypnosis. Both

states are responsive to suggestion. Tell a subject of hypnosis that he has been flung into the sea, and though standing on a dry stage, he will swim for his life. He is not pretending; he sees the engulfing waves. And even after he has been snapped out of his trance, the power of posthypnotic suggestion can affect his conduct long after.

So it was with the girls. The question "Doth Goody So and So afflict thee?" presently evoked a vivid picture of Goody So and So on the attack, and they cried out her name and the details of her misconduct. Nor were they pretending. They saw the woman.

So long as the girls accused only the lowly and people of ill repute, no one doubted them. But the next charge was against a church member in good standing, one who never missed a meeting — Martha Cory — and this caused consternation. To be sure Martha had never been popular. Others than the girls resented her self-righteousness, and now it was rumored that she was skeptical about the witchcraft itself. Nevertheless the congregation had given her the right hand of fellowship and she had to be given a chance to clear herself. Before a warrant was sworn out for her arrest, two church members, Edward Putnam and Ezekiel Cheever, undertook a private investigation.

First they visited young Ann, and in the interest of correct identification asked her to describe what Martha was wearing. Ann looked fixedly into space and shook her head. "I am blind now, I cannot see. She knows you are coming and has put me under a spell."

Martha herself, looking up from her spinning wheel when the men came, promptly confirmed Ann's words. "I know what you have come for," she said. "You are come to talk to me about being a witch. Did she tell you what clothes I have on?"

When her callers admitted that Ann could not do so, Martha laughed, as they reported later, "as if she had shown us a pretty trick." How, they asked each other, could she have known if the devil had not instructed her? Very simply. Though Martha had not attended the hearings, she knew from Giles that the question about clothes was standard with the magistrates. Now and thereafter it was regularly asked as a test of the accuracy of spectral vision. Witches had no special costume for their pranks; they went about in what they ordinarily wore.

"I do not believe that there are witches," Martha said, giving utterance to outright heresy. Reminded that three witches had already been taken, she dismissed them scornfully and asked what such as they had to do with her, a professor of the faith, a "gospel woman." Such self-righteousness exasperated her well-meaning guests.

"Woman, outward profession of faith cannot save you!" they exclaimed and left. Nevertheless she was not immediately accused. The interview took place on March 12, following the day of fasting and prayer. Not until a week later was a warrant sworn out, and since it could not be served until Monday, March 21, Martha was given an opportunity for a prodigious display of her powers before Sabbath meeting.

66

How dared she show herself there? Everyone knew about the warrant, and that but for the accident of its arriving too late to be served on a Saturday, Martha would now be awaiting her examination in jail. Unthinkable for one under charge of a diabolical crime to join godly company.

Martha walked into the meetinghouse with head held high and took her usual place. She had an answer to those who remonstrated with her: "I will open the eyes of the magistrates and ministers."

The minister this Sunday was not Parris but his predecessor Deodat Lawson, the one minister Salem Village had had to date who had not quarreled with his parishioners. The latter were grateful to him for coming in this hour of need. But they were to have great difficulty in hearing his two sermons, morning and afternoon.

Lawson had come the day before to put up at the ordinary of good Deacon Ingersoll. There Mary Walcott greeted him, or tried to. She was interrupted by a witch who bit her on the wrist. "Looking on it with a candle we saw apparently the marks of teeth, both upper and lower set, on each side of her wrist."

The word "apparently," inserted in the notes that Lawson began to take at once, suggested a certain caution in his approach to the witchcraft. He had been drawn to the village to investigate rumors that the death of his wife and child some years earlier had been caused by diabolical intervention. Having previously accepted his loss as the will of God, he was not to be convinced otherwise without proof.

But if he had some reservations about Mary, he had none about Abigail Williams when he saw her later in full cry at the parsonage. Deacon Ingersoll's wife was trying to hold the child down, but there was no restraining her. One moment she ran about flapping her arms as if trying to fly, saying "Whish! Whish!" Another, she rushed into the fireplace, made as if about to fly up the chimney, then scattered burning brands about the kitchen.

What really appalled the visiting pastor was a quieter moment when the child stood staring into the invisible world, and using both hands, strove with all her might to push something away from her.

"I won't, I won't, I won't take it!" shrieked the child. "I don't know what book it is. I am sure it is none of God's book. It is the devil's book for aught I know."

Nor was the devil's book being thrust upon the innocent child the worst of it. Abigail called out the name of the bearer. "Do you not see her? Why there she stands!" He did not see her, but he shuddered at the name. It was not Martha Cory's but that of another dame, whom during his pastorate he had deemed holy.

After the struggle with the firebrands and the invisible spirit and the deadly book would the child have the strength to attend meeting next morning? She would. She also had the strength to disrupt it.

"After psalm was sung," reported the minister, going on with his note-taking, "Abigail Williams said to me,

'Now stand up and name your text.' And after it was read she said, 'It's a long text.' "

She was not alone in her interruption. The other girls were there, and a young matron newly afflicted, a Mrs. Pope; and all had "sore fits . . . which something interrupted me in my first prayer." Only Martha Cory sat unmoved, awaiting her chance to "open the eyes" of all concerned.

She attended the afternoon service and threatened it with bedlam. Her physical presence sat quietly enough, but her shape apparently did otherwise, and Abigail's sharp eyes caught her at it.

"Look where Goody Cory sits on the beam sucking her yellow bird betwixt her fingers," she shrilled, and everyone looked. Little Ann also saw the yellow bird. It had flown from beam to the minister's hat "as it hung on the pin in the pulpit." Ann jumped up to make her announcement, but someone pulled her down and hushed her.

There were some who recalled that Abigail had always been given to wriggling in meeting, and she now took advantage of her condition to do what she had always longed to do, break up the tedium of the sermon and turn all eyes from the pulpit to her. Others who remembered the wriggling ascribed it to an early symptom of the present diabolical infestation.

Next day at the stroke of noon, Martha stood before the magistrates, prepared to open their eyes. She had to wait until the conclusion of a "very pertinent and pathetical prayer" by Nicholas Noyes, pastor of the First

Church of Salem, who had accompanied the magistrates to the village. Then she asked leave to offer a prayer of her own.

A gasp at her effrontery went over the packed meetinghouse. It is not permitted a woman to offer prayer in public; the gospel is very explicit on this point. "The magistrates told her they came there not to hear her pray, but to examine her in what was alleged against her."

"Why do you afflict these children?" then asked Magistrate Hathorne.

"I do not afflict them."

"Who doth?"

"I do not know. How should I know?"

But the girls were there and her power over them was for all to see. As Cotton Mather reported of another witch in another connection. "There was little occasion to prove the witchcraft, it being evident and notorious to all beholders."

The magistrates now witnessed what they had not seen before: the ability of the witch to afflict through the slightest gesture. Whatever move Martha made immediately tormented the girls. When she bit her lips, they bit theirs until the blood came; when she clasped her hands, they shrieked with the pain she inflicted on theirs; when she moved her feet, they set up a stamping that shook the meetinghouse.

One onlooker, a young matron who had come not to testify but to observe, was caught in this witch's toils, for hysteria, though caused by no virus, is the most contagious of diseases. It lies at the root of all mob madness, when otherwise sane people trample each other in panic at the cry of fire, or join a lynching. It was so that Gertrude Pope caught the torments of the girls. When Martha wearily leaned against the back of a chair, she was seized with such a pain in her bowels that she flung her shoe and struck Martha on the side of her head.

Meanwhile Martha, so confident of her power to bring the community to its senses by reasoning with it, was getting small opportunity to make herself heard at all.

"I have no familiarity with any such thing," she retorted to the charge that she sucked a yellow bird between her fingers. "I am a gospel woman."

"Gospel witch! Gospel witch!" shrieked the girls.

Ann Putnam reported having seen her pray to the devil.

"Nay," said Martha. "We must not heed these poor distracted children."

Distracted children, indeed. Who distracted them? "You càn't prove me a witch!" she cried just before she was led off to the Salem jail. What she could not do under these circumstances was prove that she was not.

7

Like all sensible people, the family of Francis and Rebecca Nurse believed in witchcraft. Theirs was a large family: four sons, four daughters, and since all but one of the latter had married, three sons-in-law. They were a united family. All lived in or close by the Townsend-Bishop house, one of the oldest and finest in the village, and all worked together to make the yearly payments on the fruitful acres cut out from the Endicott property.

They had some problems. Old Zerubabul Endicott, who lived nearby at Orchard Farm, objected to their purchase, in which he had no part, and once sent his hands to keep them out of a woodlot both claimed. There had been a scrimmage, and it did not please him that the Nurses had won. Another neighbor named Holton failed to mend his section of the fence between their property, and his hogs got through and destroyed Rebecca's precious flax garden. Rebecca, gentlest of dames, had gone into a rage and denounced poor

Benjamin Holton in terms not gentle at all. When he died not long after, his wife held Rebecca responsible.

But for all the resentment in some quarters of the family's prosperity, and the unspoken wish that just once they would default on their payments, none could deny that they were upright citizens, paying their church rates and now supporting the proper prosecution of the witchcraft. One son-in-law, Thomas Preston, had put his name on the first warrants.

He had no compunction in doing so. Sarah Good was a nuisance and a witch if he ever saw one; the others were no better. But when the accusations swung around to his revered mother-in-law, he saw things in a different light. Knowing that the charges had originated with little Ann Putnam, he and his brother-in-law John Tarbell went to question the child.

The visit was well timed. All the Putnam females, the two Anns and Mercy Lewis, were enjoying a respite of good health. Even the elder Ann, whom Deodat Lawson had recently seen near death in her torments, was having a lucid interval. But the errand was to her daughter.

"Ann, was it not you who accused my mother before the others spoke?" asked Tarbell.

Young Ann looked up at him with truthful eyes and searched her mind for the pictures that flickered so often through it. She spoke carefully.

"I saw the apparition of a pale-faced woman that sat in her grandmother seat. I did not know her name."

"Who named her then?"

"Goody Putnam did!" cried out Mercy Lewis.

"Mercy named her!" shouted the elder Ann.

Watching the scene with stern eyes, Tarbell prepared to make a deposition to the magistrates in case of need. "Thus they turned it upon one another, saying it was you, it was you that named her."

Young Ann said nothing. Her tranced eyes were fixed on the unseen. Again she saw the pale-faced woman in her grandmother chair, and now something else. She saw her join Martha Cory in her prayers to the evil one. She was still not sure of her identity. But if her mother knew her as Rebecca Nurse, that was who it was. Later, much later, Ann would recall her uncertainty, and experience remorse for the affliction she had brought upon the Nurse family. For, two days after Martha, Rebecca herself faced the magistrates.

The magistrates, like most of the villagers, were horrified that accusation had turned from people of ill repute to church members in good standing. This sentiment probably accounted for the delay in swearing out a warrant against Martha Cory. She was not well liked, but the congregation had after all freely given her the right hand of fellowship. Now here was a second "professor" accused, and from Tarbell's testimony the magistrates knew that young Ann Putnam who saw her first could not name her until her mother did.

And what ground for suspicion did the elder Ann have against Rebecca? It obviously went back to the troubled ministry of her brother-in-law Bayley. Rebecca had not, like most of the parish, changed her affiliation to the Salem Village church; she was still a member of the congregation in Salem Town. She may well have belonged to the dissident minority that protested the calling of James Bayley. With or without reason, the elder Ann connected her with the spying and gossip that had made her sister's life at the parsonage so miserable.

There was another circumstance. Some members of the Putnam family now remembered that there had been talk that Rebecca's mother, Mary Towne, had dabbled in witchcraft — on what ground the talk was based was never explained. Perhaps it was only her knowledge of herbs brought with her from the old country, perhaps her skill in forecasting storms. Or it may have been an incident of "mischief following anger," like the death of Rebecca's neighbor after she flew out at him for letting his hogs get into her garden. The elder Ann had for years been looking for the source of her miseries, and when her daughter saw the vision of the old woman, all the pieces fitted together.

The magistrates were prepared to deal with Rebecca gently. She was old and frail and recently come from her sickbed. Nor was there in her any of the self-righteousness that had antagonized them when they had Martha Cory before them. Rebecca's plea got a sympathetic hearing.

"I can say before my eternal father that I am innocent and God will clear my innocence."

"Here is never a one in the assembly but desires it," said Hathorne. He had been talking with his sister, Elizabeth Porter. She and her husband Isaac had visited Rebecca on the same errand that had taken others to

Martha. They had found in her none of Martha's incriminating prescience. She had anxiously inquired after the afflicted girls, whom she would have visited but for her illness. Then she had spoken, it would seem, of the charges against Martha.

"I am troubled at some of their crying out. Some of the persons they have spoken of are, as I believe, as innocent as I."

It was then that the Porters brought themselves to the point of their visit, Rebecca had been accused. She was very deaf. They had to repeat before she grasped what they said. Then she was stricken beyond speech.

"Well if it be so, the will of the Lord be done," said the old woman at last; and then a cry was wrung from her heart. "As to this thing I am innocent as the child unborn. But surely what sin hath God found in me unrepented of that He could lay such affliction on me in my old age?"

These words rang in Magistrate Hathorne's ears as if he had been with his sister, and that God would clear her innocence he could well believe. Nevertheless he felt obliged to add, "But if you be guilty, I pray God discover you," and began to take evidence. Edward Putnam reported that she had tortured his niece Ann in his presence.

"I am innocent and clear and have not been able to get out of doors these eight — nine days," replied Rebecca to this. She had not yet grasped that not her physical body but her spectral shape was involved in such deeds. "I never afflicted no child, no never in my life."

The magistrate could well believe it. "Are you," he now asked, "an innocent person relating to this witchcraft?"

Deodat Lawson, who had left the meetinghouse after the opening prayers to work on his lecture day sermon, was stopped in his tracks by the clamor that then arose. "Such a hideous screech and noise as did amaze me, and some that were within told me the whole assembly was struck with consternation, and they were afraid that those that sat next to them were under the influence of witchcraft."

The girls, quiet at first, had gone into full possession. Hathorne's words had suggested doubt. It was now given the girls to "discover" Rebecca's guilt. And they did it in such tumult that Parris, who was acting as court reporter, got hopelessly behind in his note-taking.

"Oh God help me!" cried Rebecca and wrung her hands. Fatal gesture, for now as with Martha Cory every move she made was mimicked by the girls. In view of the whole village she practiced her diabolical powers. The magistrate repented his weakness.

"You would do well if you are guilty to confess," he said sternly.

But Rebecca, hardly able to stand, seldom able to hear what was said to her through the confusion and her deafness, did not waver in her testimony.

"Would you have me belie myself?" she asked.

Her very deafness became a charge against her. The girls detected its cause: the Black Man was whispering in her ear. The elder Ann was prepared to charge her with multiple murder. She did not do it today because she was taken with such a "grievous fit" that "she could hardly move hand or foot," and had to be carried out. Later she would record testimony that she had from her daughter. The younger Ann had lately shared her mother's recurrent dream. She too saw the dead babies; they held out their hands to her, called her aunt, and cried out the name of their murderer: Goody Nurse.

That came later. Today through all the clamor, through all her weakness, Rebecca finally grasped the nature of the evidence against her, the so called "spectral evidence."

"The devil," she said, "may appear in my shape."

This to the magistrates was no defense at all. They had been sifting through the rules of evidence in witchcraft and had found it a cardinal principle that the innocent could not be falsely represented. Rebecca Nurse was sent to the jail in Salem until she could be removed to Boston.

A very small witch joined her in both places. The magistrates had at first dismissed as improbable Ann Putnam's charge against little Dorcas Good. But lately she had taken to biting nearly everyone. The girls, reported Lawson, "produced the marks of small teeth accordingly."

Dorcas was five, an age of fantasy. To questions, she willingly answered that her mother had made her a witch and had given her a "familiar." Witch lore was full of familiars — turtles, yellow birds, cats, in this case a small snake. What such creatures did for the witch was never made clear, but they did much for the magistrates, for it was known that they were suckled on the witch's body. One part of every examination, conducted privately by members of the appropriate sex, was a search of the body of the accused for "witch-marks." No need to search Dorcas. She displayed a red spot about the "bigness" of a fleabite on the knuckle of a forefinger. It was there that she suckled her snake.

Soon after, the three in Boston jail got other company, and Tituba had a child to console her for her separation from Betty. Dorcas was, according to Lawson, "hale and well looking," but she would not remain so long. Tituba did what she could, cuddled the child, sang to her, tried to untangle the snarls in her yellow hair with her fingers for want of other implement, and wished she had with her the "lice comb" she had sometimes used on Betty. But these were grim quarters, and when after a year the child was let out into daylight again, she was like a hunted, wild thing.

From her mother she got little attention. Goody Good had her pipe with her, and when visitors came to look through the bars as at a zoo, she begged tobacco of them.

"There's tobacco good enough for you!" cried one girl, and thrust wood shavings through the bars. Sarah cursed her, and the fits of the girl, whose name was Mercy Short, gave Cotton Mather a subject for his investigations.

79

8

The latest arrests had profoundly disturbed and divided the community. Likable or not, Martha Cory was no one's idea of a witch, and foisting such a charge on Rebecca Nurse was, to those who knew her best, simply preposterous. Already her friends were collecting signatures on a statement that in all the years of their acquaintance they had never detected the least sign of evil in her conduct.

It was for the ministers to address themselves to this doubt. Deodat Lawson took on that duty in the lecture day sermon he had been preparing while Rebecca faced her accusers.

"It is certain that the devil never works more like the Prince of Darkness than when he looks most like an angel of light," he explained. "I thus am commanded to call and cry to you Arm! Arm! Let us admit no parley."

On the first Sunday in April, sacrament day in the village, Parris resumed his place in the pulpit, and following Lawson's lead, selected an appropriate text:

"Have I not chosen you twelve and one of you is a devil?"

He had barely completed this reading, dwelling on each syllable with sonorous emphasis, when there was an unseemly interruption. It came not from the girls — even Abigail sat quietly today — but from a matron in her fifties. She suddenly rose, marched to the rear door and closed it with a crash behind her.

When the clatter died down, Parris made a solemn comment: "Christ knows how many devils there are in his church and who they are."

The woman was Sarah Cloyce, the younger of Rebecca's two sisters. She shared the resentment of the entire Nurse family against a pastor who took guilt for granted in disregard of a long life of charity and good report. But if she seemed to leave the church in temper, her friends made anxious excuses: a sudden illness had caused her to go; far from slamming the door behind her, the wind had snatched it from her hand.

She had, however, fatally drawn the attention of the girls. When they came out of the meetinghouse after the sacrament, they found a coven of witches, invisible to everyone else, on the lawn, mocking holy religion with their own sacrament of red bread and·blood, and Sarah Cloyce was among them.

A week later, brought before the magistrates, her temper flared out again. It was directed at John Indian, a recent recruit to the company of the afflicted, who writhing and tumbling at her feet, accused her of tormenting him "many times."

"Oh you are a grievous liar!" cried Sarah.

It did her no good; everyone could see what she was doing to poor John Indian.

"It's no wonder they are witches, their mother was a witch before them," remarked Ann's uncle, John Putnam. He should have held his tongue. That night his healthy eight-weeks-old baby was stricken and died in agony in spite of Dr. Grigg's helpless ministrations. He had no doubt of the cause.

But the division in the community extended to the Putnam family. Joseph went to the house of his elder half brother and spoke wickedly to his sister-in-law.

"If you dare to touch with your foul lies anyone belonging to my household, you shall answer for it!"

The elder Ann was silent. It was her daughter who answered him.

"My mother does not belie herself," was all she said, but looking into the fixed stare of her eyes, the eyes of a Delphic sybil, her uncle was afraid. Incredible to fear a child whom not long ago he had rocked on his knee and taught to play cat's cradle, but afraid he was. He rode home and did not unsaddle his horse. Presently it was rumored that night and day he kept one horse saddled in his stable, ready for flight.

The girls themselves fell into division. There was something like a generation gap among them; when the magistrates spoke of "the afflicted children," they disregarded the two eldest, Sarah Churchill and Mary Warren, both in their twenties. These two had nothing in common with the youngest children and did not share the intimacies of the teen-agers. Living farther out of the village than the others, they were separated not only by age but distance. And each was subject to a master who was skeptical of their fits and the visions they saw in them.

Sarah Churchill did not relish being called a "bitch witch" by her master George Jacobs. The phrase afflicted her. She reported and demonstrated the affliction but when her reports led to her master's arrest and she heard his peppery retorts to the magistrates, something happened to her. The girls, she began to say, "did but dissemble."

Such heresy in turn afflicted the girls. They accused her, and Sarah herself was brought to court. She got herself out of trouble only by "confessing." Yes, she had signed the book when her master and another witch forced it on her.

Later she repudiated her confession. To a trusted friend she sobbed out her story and made accusations against the Salem minister, Nicholas Noyes. "If I told him a hundred times I was innocent, he would not believe me. But if I said once I signed that book he believed." In the interest of truth the friend reported the incident to the magistrates, but they brushed it aside.

They could not so easily brush aside the strange statements made by Mary Warren.

When her master John Procter had exclaimed of the girls, "Hang them! They'll make witches of us all," he had spoken truly. Soon after the arrest of Rebecca Nurse, his wife was accused. An incident in Ingersoll's ordinary seems to have precipitated the accusation.

"There goes Goody Procter!" cried one of the girls. "Old witch, I'll have her hang."

This took place before witnesses of more than usual common sense. They looked about them, saw nothing, and told the girl they believed she lied.

"It was for sport," stammered the girl. She seemed to have forgotten the distinction between bodily presence and spectral shape. "I must have sport."

But there were later accusations. Though Procter himself stood high in the community, it was known that his wife had Quaker connections, and in good Puritan eyes there had always been something witchlike about Quakers. She was brought before the magistrates on April 11, and made a gentle reply to an accusation by Abigail Williams.

"Dear child, it is not so," she said. "There is another judgment, dear child."

Procter had come to stand by his wife. Not physically, for that was not allowed, no matter how feeble the accused, but by raising the voice of common sense. After one of his remarks the dear child Abigail turned on him. "Why he can pinch as well as she!" she cried.

Then the girls went into full cry. Parris, who had again taken the job of court reporter, found it impossible to keep his notes in order. Only Mary Walcott was calm. She had her knitting with her and worked steadily, looking up occasionally to report. She warned John Indian that Procter was astride him.

Like Martha Cory, Procter had hoped to "open the eyes" of the magistrates. He was no more successful than

84

she. Their attention was centered not on his protest but on the contortions and shrieks of the girls.

"You see the devil will deceive you," one magistrate said sternly. "The children could see what you was going to do before the woman was hurt. I would advise you to repentance, for the devil is bringing you out." And they remanded him with his wife to Salem jail until they could be shipped to Boston.

His "jade" Mary Warren may or may not have joined the clamor of the other girls. Caught up in the general hysteria she could not help herself. But when the pandemonium ended she had sobering thoughts. Accusing Betty Procter was one thing, but her master, no. These thoughts were reinforced when the constable came to the Procter home and seized everything that could be carried away, so that there was not even a mug for the children to drink from. At this point she joined the skeptics who said "the girls did but dissemble."

She said other things too. "The magistrates might as well examine the keeper's daughter that had been distracted many years, and take notice of what she said as any of the afflicted persons."

She recounted her own experience. "When I was afflicted I thought I saw the apparitions of a hundred persons, for my head was distempered, and I could not tell what I said. When I was well again, I could not say that I saw any of the apparitions at the time aforesaid."

These remarks were made not to the magistrates but to her fellow prisoners in Salem jail. Her defection had troubled the girls, and they lost no time in accusing her. Now she faced the magistrates.

"You were a little while ago an afflicted person," said Hathorne. "Now you are an afflicter. How comes this to pass?"

If Mary had been permitted counsel she might have found a proper answer. But the Puritans had a low opinion of the legal profession and gave none of those accused of the witchcraft the right of counsel. Mary stammered out an improbable reply.

"I look up to God and I take it to be a mercy of God."

"What! Do you take it as a mercy to afflict others?"

What to say to that? What would her master have said? But he was far away and the girls yowling in their fits were near, and their commotion contagious. Mary sank to the floor.

"I will speak!" she cried. "Oh I am sorry for it. I am sorry for it. Oh Lord help me. Oh good Lord save me. I will tell! I will tell!"

Tell what? Was the sanity of John Procter trying to make itself heard in the voice of this distracted girl? Distracted she was. Her panic brought on a fit so severe that she had to be carried out, and thereafter the magistrates interviewed her in the fastness of Salem jail. If she spoke to them as to her fellow prisoners, they did not record it. They accepted her "confession" at last, but only in the terms of the prevailing fantasy.

Eventually she accused again, and it was always Betty Procter whom she accused. She had found "poppets" about the house, a plausible statement since the Procters had small children to play with dolls. But when Betty stuck a pin into one of these poppets, one of the girls immediately felt the pain.

She accused Betty Procter of such ill temper that her husband sometimes thought of making way with himself. The evil wife attacked her in the presence of the magistrates, who saw her fighting her off. "She saith she will kill me. Oh she saith she owes me a spite and will claw me off. Avoid Satan, for the name of God avoid."

Only late in the day did she report a vision which involved her master. She felt a shape hovering above her, pulled it down, and there was John Procter in her lap.

It was at this point that Mary was considered free of her sins and permitted to rejoin the circle of the afflicted. But her part thereafter was apparently limited to demonstration, to responses to what was to be called "the touch test." If she spoke again, no record was made. More and more the magistrates were relying on the word of a child, the younger Ann Putnam.

9

What inspired confidence in young Ann was her utter truthfulness. Never would she speak in "sport." In the seriousness of her quest she had forgotten what sport was. Nor did the spirits that afflicted her have the trickiness of those that beset little Abigail, who reveled in a license to commit outrageous mischief.

Her purpose was dead serious: to uncover the deviltries that had tormented her mother even before she was born. Her mother was often possessed, the maidservant Mercy Lewis even more often, but when Ann spoke out of her trances, the whole family hung on her words.

"Oh dreadful, dreadful! Here is a minister come!" she cried one day. She was staring into the pasture assigned to the Reverend Samuel Parris, whom the witches took pleasure in mocking by assembling there to hold their "Sabbaths." "What, are ministers witches too?"

Who was he? She could not remember having seen him either in the flesh or spectrally. He resembled, however, the "little black minister" of whom Tituba had spoken. Bravely she questioned him.

"Oh dreadful, dreadful, tell me your name that I may know who you are," and repeated her demand until the minister not only told her his name but boasted that "he was above a witch for he was a conjurer." But the spirit wanted no publicity. When in the privacy of her home Ann tried to speak, he choked her nearly to death. Not until a "shining spirit," recognizable from the book of Revelation, came to her rescue, was she relieved and able to give voice.

The name so shocked her father that he dared not include it in a note he promptly wrote to the magistrates "to inform Your Honors of what we conceive you have not heard, which are high and dreadful . . . of a wheel within a wheel at which our ears do tingle."

When he informed the magistrates in person, the specter was seen by others, including Abigail. This minister had become the grand wizard of all Massachusetts, and not only did he preside over the covens in the pasture but in the past he had killed, among others, the wife of Deodat Lawson.

So it happened that early in May the Reverend George Burroughs, who hadn't visited his former parish for more than a decade, saw it again. The magistrates sent all the way to the frontier settlement of Wells in Maine to fetch him. He was sitting at table with his wife (his third; according to the seeresses of Salem Village he had murdered her two predecessors) when he was snatched way, not even given a chance to finish his bread and cheese.

That young Ann had truly seen him in the devil's service is certain. Her imagination had always been vivid and under the stress of the witch-hunt she had lost the distinction between fantasy and reality. The name the shape told her was already present under the surface of her consciousness; her mother had often spoken of this minister. It was he who over her sick baby's cradle had talked of God's will.

It had been Burroughs's misfortune to follow Bayley in the pastorate. It was no doing of his that Bayley had left, but partisans of the latter resented him furiously. If it had been possible to recruit one of the apostles to succeed Bayley, neither Matthew, Mark, Luke nor John could have given satisfaction.

He had friends, however. Good Deacon Ingersoll had come to his rescue when he was arrested for failing to pay part of one wife's funeral expenses. Now, while he awaited examination in a private home in Salem, an admirer proclaimed, "I believe he is a choice child of God and that God will clear his innocency," and prevailed on an acquaintance to visit him out of Christian charity.

He should have let well enough alone. Right after the visit the reluctant caller was troubled with visions, "something like jelly" that did "quaver with a strange motion," and his testimony was introduced as one more count against the minister.

Burroughs was not at once introduced to the society

of the afflicted girls. The ministry was profoundly disturbed that one of their number should be accused, and held private conferences with him before delivering him to the magistrates. They got some damaging admissions: he could not remember when he had last served the Lord's Supper, and of his seven children only the eldest son had been baptized. He "owned that there were toads" in his house in Maine. A toad might well have been his familiar, suckled somewhere on his body, but when he was searched no witch-mark was found.

Cotton Mather had no part in the ministers' conference, but he eagerly collected details in preparation for writing his history of the witchcraft. He was especially impressed by Burroughs's prowess as an athlete. Mather had learned to read almost as early as he learned to walk, and his youth had been exclusively bookish. Given his background, the wonder tales of Burroughs's power to lift and carry heavy weights were one more proof of diabolism. "He was a puny man, yet he had often done things beyond the strength of a giant."

The examination began on May 9 before not two but four magistrates. Judge Samuel Sewall had come up from Boston, and with him the distinguished Judge William Stoughton, soon to take office as deputy governor under the new Massachusetts charter. He presided as chief magistrate, but in conducting the hearing he made use of the experience of Corwin and Hathorne.

The function of the hearing was not only to take testimony but to observe the effect of Burroughs's presence upon the girls. He was at first not permitted to look their way. They sat quietly, invisibly as far as he was concerned, until he was directed to turn his head to them. The poor man was aghast at the pandemonium that then ensued.

"What think you of that?" sternly asked Stoughton.

"It is an amazing and humbling Providence," stammered the accused, "but I understand nothing of it." Then he collected his wits, studied the girls, and sorted out their cries from the prevailing clamor. It led him to an observation. "When they begin to name my name they cannot name it."

"What hinders them?" demanded Stoughton.

"I suppose it is the devil."

Stoughton pounced. "How comes the devil then to be so loath to have any testimony borne against you?" In his confusion Burroughs could not answer.

Mercy Lewis made herself heard above the clamor. She had seen a "new fashioned" book in Burroughs's study, and he had pressed her to sign it. Burroughs stared at her. When had this strapping wench been in his study and permitted to meddle with his precious store of books? Then he caught her name and remembered. In her childhood, Mercy had served for a time in his household.

She had more to say. Out of a trance she reported that Burroughs had carried her upon a very high mountain where he "showed her mighty and glorious kingdoms and said he would give them all to her if she would write in his book." Did this wench, wondered Burroughs, confound herself with Christ in His temptations? At least she had listened to his sermons.

The girls interrupted her testimony with shrieks of pain. The wizard was biting them. They held up their hands to show the bites, and the magistrates made a dental inspection. They examined Burroughs's teeth, then each others', and looked again at the arms of the girls. They were telling the truth; only Burroughs's teeth could have produced these marks.

He not only bit, he slew. Hysterically little Ann reported what the apparitions of his first two wives had told her, his barbarous treatment and then their deaths at his hand. Then she fell into a fit so severe that she had to be removed. It was also reported that he had killed the wife and child of his successor Deodat Lawson, out of jealousy that Lawson had pleased the parish when he could not. And when Lawson's son went "to the eastward" to fight the Indians, not they but Burroughs had killed him.

He heard himself accused of nearly every mischief committed by the Indians on the Maine frontier. Late in January, after the raid on York which had so upset Mary Walcott, he had written an urgent appeal for help to the governor and council. "God is still manifesting His displeasure against this land. He who formerly hath set His hand to help us doth even write bitter things against us." Now he heard that not the Indians but he was responsible for that plight.

There were "confessing witches," in Salem jail now, women who after vainly pleading their innocence on the stand, gave up in fright, weariness and utter confusion, and told the magistrates everything they wanted to hear, following the lead of Tituba. These were now interviewed, among them Mary Warren, who had not yet restored herself to the ranks of the afflicted, and they confirmed that Burroughs had been made the wizard of all Massachusetts. It was he who sounded the trumpet for the meetings in Parris's pasture, where he was served by his deacons, Rebecca Nurse and John Procter.

At last the hearing was over, the clamor stilled. In the comparative peace of his cell, first in Salem, then in Boston, the "little black minister" sorted out his impressions, wrote letters to his children and applied himself to dispel the strange delusion that had come upon Massachusetts.

10

In spite of the vigor with which the witchcraft had been prosecuted, there were difficulties embarrassing to the magistrates. They had conducted hearings only, inquests as it were. There had been no trials, and without trials there could be no hangings.

These were becoming urgently necessary, if only for the safety of the girls. Only the bodily presence of a witch could be jailed. Some of those in confinement still sent out their shapes to bedevil their victims. Once they were hanged, that power would cease, or so the magistrates reasoned. There was to be a notable exception, one of the most curious incidents in the witchcraft, but that they could not foresee.

Another reason for action was the impossible overcrowding of the jails. Accusations and arrests had multiplied. All Essex County was now involved, and some adjacent communities. One deputy constable had been accused of witchcraft. In March, John Willard had willingly cooperated in the arrest of the likes of Sarah Good, but when he was called to take up people he respected, he exclaimed, "Hang them! They're all witches," rebelled and fled. He was accused, overtaken, and was now among those being held for trial.

It did not contribute to the dignity of government that some of the more frivolous townspeople of Boston regarded the jail as a kind of sideshow set up for their entertainment. Nor did it contribute to public safety. Cotton Mather was having an arduous time curing Mercy Short of the fits brought on by Sarah Good.

Why the delay in bringing the prisoners to trial? It was the uneasy condition of the Bay Colony, which for the time being lay helpless between two governments. The old charter, under which it had governed itself almost like an independent state since 1630, had been revoked, and the new one, which Cotton Mather's father Increase had been sent to England to negotiate, had not yet arrived. Massachusetts was in a state of limbo: without legal authority to conduct such trials, without knowledge of the form they must take.

It did have a governor. Simon Bradstreet held that office until the royal pleasure could be learned. But he was close to ninety, and lately so enfeebled by illness that he had not been able to attend Sabbath meeting, much less the examinations. Some considered his incapacity a tragedy, some a blessing, for Bradstreet was known to be soft on witchcraft. He had refused to hang one condemned during his earlier administration.

But what to do? Fortunately the waiting came to an end. Less than a week after Burroughs faced the magistrates, the good ship *Nonesuch* reached Boston, carrying

Increase Mather, the new charter, and Sir William Phips, the governor appointed by William and Mary. The charter did not confirm the old privileges, and a governor by royal appointment was a humiliation to a people used to electing their own. But there was some comfort in that Phips was a New Englander born and bred, and for better or worse this was a government. Soon after Phips's arrival, the magistrates learned that the trials could be conducted in the court of Oyer and Terminer.

No one was more eager for the trials than the most intelligent and resolute of the accused. To "witches" like Martha Cory, John Procter, Rebecca Nurse and her sisters (her second sister, Mary Esty, had been arrested after Sarah Cloyce) it was inconceivable that the trial judges would accept the sort of evidence used in the hearings. Procter was working to induce the ministers of Boston to investigate these procedures. He had sent them a petition describing the tortures used to force confessions from accused men (one his eldest son) and protesting the use of spectral evidence. Increase Mather, startled on his return from England to find the colony overrun with witches, would presently make such a study.

But the first trial, of Bridget Bishop on June 2, was a blow to such hopes. The girls were brought to court in Salem to demonstrate the touch test, and even more damaging evidence than their contortions was the testimony of grown men. In her youth, Bridget Bishop obviously had a powerful attraction for the opposite sex;

she haunted their dreams. Not that it was so reported, for no more than the girls did these men distinguish between dream and reality. What they swore was that at midnight or just before dawn she came through their windows, not bodily, but as a "shape," and being repulsed, inflicted great injury on themselves and their children.

What in the face of such proof could the judges do but sentence her to hang? Then there was a delay. Not until General Court revived an old law making witchcraft a capital crime, did the hanging take place — on June 8.

There was some comfort in the fact that this witch was a character of much notoriety. It was not the first time she had been charged as a witch. Several years earlier her minister, John Hale of Beverly, had saved her by convincing the court that a woman she had supposedly done to death by her spells was deranged and a suicide.

She conducted two taverns on the North Shore where shovel-board was played so noisily that it disturbed the neighbors. She was a flashy dresser, fond of laces which she had dyed, and often seen both in the bodily presence and spectrally in a "red paragon bodice." Gossiped about for decades, what had she in common with the likes of Rebecca Nurse or of John Procter? For the latter, not only his present neighbors but most of the town of Ipswich, his former home, were getting together a petition on his behalf.

When, on June 28, Rebecca came to trial their hopes seemed justified. After listening to the familiar rigmarole and watching the antics of the girls, the jury brought in a verdict of not guilty.

The announcement came from the foreman, Thomas Fisk. He had braced himself for the reaction of the girls, who promptly fell screaming and writhing to the floor. There was nothing new in that, except perhaps in degree. The whole trial, like that of Bridget Bishop, had been accompanied by their yowling. After a time a man of steady nerve could get accustomed to it as one might to the din in a boiler factory.

But if he did not flinch before the clamor, he did before the cold eye of Chief Justice Stoughton.

The latter had no legal training and no knowledge of the law beyond that set down in the manuals on witchcraft. He had been trained as a minister, and during the period of Cromwell's Commonwealth had so served in England. That under the law a judge must accept without question a jury's verdict of not guilty did not occur to him. He did not accept; he challenged.

Had the jury, he asked, taken into consideration an incriminating remark made by Rebecca. "When Deliverance Hobbs was brought into court to testify, the prisoner, turning her head to her, said, 'What, do you bring her? She is one of us.' Has the jury weighed the implications of that statement?"

Fisk hesitated. He recalled the testimony of Deliverance Hobbs, one of the prisoners who had collapsed into confession after vainly asserting her innocence, but he could not remember Rebecca's remark. He turned to consult the jury, and finding their memories as blank as his, he came back to court to ask Rebecca what she had said and what she meant by it.

The old woman still stood at the bar, clinging to it for support. Her strength had lately been taxed beyond endurance, and the worst was still ahead of her. If she was found guilty she would be taken into the Salem meetinghouse to receive a sentence of excommunication. She would be given one more chance to give glory to God and confess. Glory she would give to God as long as breath remained in her body, but confess to what she had not done she would not.

She stood trembling at the bar, so overcome that she did not see the man who came to question her. So many had come and gone. Nor did she through the racket and her deafness hear the question.

Earnestly Fisk repeated it. She said nothing, and the fixity of her gaze that looked past him was disturbing. There was indeed something witchlike about it, as if she were looking into the invisible world. He took her silence for an admission of guilt. When Fisk brought the jury back into court, Stoughton got the verdict he wanted: guilty.

Later Rebecca was made to understand what had happened and explained her silence. "Somewhat hard of hearing and full of grief," she had not heard the question. Her speaking of Deliverance Hobbs as "one of us" had referred only to her status as a fellow prisoner, not as Stoughton took it, as a fellow participant in the diabolical meetings in Parris's pasture.

She was too late to sway the jury; the verdict was in

and she was condemned to hang. Her family then went to Governor Phips with the story and persuaded him to sign a reprieve. But in reprieving Rebecca he seemed to be passing a death sentence on innocent girls. Rebecca's triumphant shape issued from prison to torment them and reduce them to extremity. When the governor heard of this, he rescinded his reprieve.

Young Ann had been one of those done nearly to death. Her whole family, standing by helplessly watching her desperate struggle to beat off diabolical attack, had seen her sink into coma. Ann was to look back at this event aghast at what she had done, and to cry out to the Nurse family for forgiveness. But that was many years later, too late to save Rebecca. On July 19 she was hanged on Gallows Hill with four others, among them Sarah Good. At the time Ann felt only a blessed release. No more would she be haunted by the murdered babes who held out their hands to her and called her aunt. By God's grace they had been avenged.

One judge did not call it God's grace. Stoughton had not sat alone on the bench. He had with him the two experienced magistrates, as well as Samuel Sewall and Nathaniel Saltonstall. The latter had been disturbed that Bridget Bishop had been condemned on nothing more tangible than hallucinations, and that Rebecca's long life of good works was disregarded on similar evidence. In protest he withdrew from the bench and retired to Haverhill, where he presently heard from Sewall that he still had faith in his integrity. For after his departure the girls had taken to accusing the absent judge.

101

11

The circle of the afflicted had undergone changes during the months of the witch-hunt. Young Abigail Williams, whose antics so impressed Deodat Lawson, seemed to be no longer present. Her last recorded public appearance had been the day after Ann named George Burroughs. The child then saw him too and danced about Ingersoll's ordinary inciting young men to slash at his specter with their swords. One effort succeeded. The child picked up a bit of cloth that she said had been cut from Burroughs's greatcoat, and reported that the floor of the ordinary was covered with the blood of slain witches invading from Connecticut.

Was that too tall a tale to convince the magistrates? Odd that an airy substance like a shape should wear something as tangible as a greatcoat. Whether they believed her or not, the child had become a nuisance at the examinations. The spirits that possessed her were of the order of the mischief-making spirits called poltergeists. Sometimes they made her rush at a recorder, to snatch the paper from under his pen and scatter his notes about the floor.

She could only be pitied; the mischief was not hers but the evil one's. However examinations could better be conducted when Abigail was somewhere else, and presently this was arranged. The villagers were too preoccupied with their own troubles, their increasingly frantic fears, to gossip about the absence of one child, but probably she had joined her cousin in Salem Town.

An uncanny quiet now returned to the parsonage. The Parrises could sleep through the night without fear that Abigail's demons would drive her to the hearth to scatter burning brands about the room. Not that it had ever happened during the night; her demons craved an audience. Of the old household only John Indian remained, and he was much in demand to wait on the guests at Ingersoll's ordinary. There he too sometimes went into possession, and between spasms took pleasure in serving the guests as a guide to the witchcraft.

He was not the only male afflicted. Sixteen-year-old John Doritch suffered fits and gave some testimony. But only briefly. Women and young girls were better at detecting spirits.

Two of the older women who had attached themselves to the circle were now seldom heard from. One was the young matron who at the Cory examination had flung her shoe at Martha's head. Goody Pope suffered a puzzled mistrust of her own visions. They had come to seem like an aberration, like the fantasies of a bad dream. She did not renounce them, much less denounce the visions of the girls still in possession; she merely fell silent.

Another woman no longer attended to was an older woman called Goody Bibber. This was not from lack of conviction on her part but from lack of trust in her testimony. Too many witnesses had reported seeing her pull pins from her bodice, stick them into her flesh, then scream that the witches had done it. The magistrates were not putting up with any chicanery.

On the other hand Mary Warren had returned from prison to rejoin the circle. At every examination she yammered and howled, and sometimes her demons dragged her about the floor and thrust her under a table. Her testimony, however, no longer carried much weight. She seemed too much like one demented, as perhaps was the case.

Many of the accused, and such of their friends as dared come to their defense, blamed the magistrates for the reliance they placed on the girls. "It is a shame that you mind these people who are out of their wits!" cried one from the stand.

The magistrates, however, collected other evidence than that supplied by the girls. They had the body of each one accused meticulously searched for witch-marks. They examined them personally on doctrinal matters, gave each a chance to repeat the Lord's Prayer. This was an important test, for the devil cannot utter words so sacred without garbling them. A witch would blunder, saying "hollowed" for hallowed, or add phrases not in Holy Writ, not at least in the King James version.

The magistrates also industriously collected proof of mischief following anger. The death of a neighbor of Rebecca Nurse, after she had given him a tongue-lashing for letting his hogs get into her flax garden, was a good example. As others were accused, any number of people came forward with reports of like mischief: a wagon wheel stuck in a hole that had vanished when the carter went back to examine it. (He had just refused to lend the accused his scythe.) Cattle had died mysteriously after the ousting of Sarah Good from her temporary home.

A whole herd of cattle was possessed into swimming from Salisbury Beach to Plum Island, most of them drowning on the way. They belonged to a man who had angered Susanna Martin by refusing to hitch up his oxen to haul her some staves. Such tales abounded about Susanna, who was sharp tongued and a Quaker. Decades before that heresy alone would have been enough to hang her. Now her neighbors went to the magistrates to give evidence of her witcheries, complete with dates.

"So that happened four and twenty years ago," remarked one Amesbury justice to a voluble accuser. "Why did you wait so long to report it?" But he made a record and sent it to Salem to be on hand when Susanna faced the girls and broke into laughter at their antics. "Well may I laugh at such folly!"

Very important was the testimony of the "confessing witches." Of these there were now an impressive number; some had collapsed into confession from sheer panic; some, especially the men, were tortured into it.

John Procter had collected a report of the methods of torture and sent it to the ministers of Boston. Some confessed to save their necks, for it was notable that contrary to the practice in England, the judges did not hang a confessing witch. At least so far they had not.

What could be better proof than what came from the confessors? They furnished homely details, of witches carrying bread and cheese to their rendezvous with the devil, of a broomstick breaking in flight and their continuing the journey by clinging for dear life to each other. Most vital of all, they named those whom they saw at the infernal rites; indeed they were not allowed to rest until they had done so. After the arrest of Burroughs every confessor agreed that he had conducted the unholy rituals they attended. Under pressure they named others still unsuspected, and in time caused more arrests than the visions of the girls.

It must have been thus that "the tall man of Boston," first seen by Tituba, was finally identified. The girls also saw him regularly, but having small acquaintance in Boston, they could not name him. It was a wily warlock who would not repeat Burroughs's folly of giving his name on request.

He turned out to be none other than John Alden, firstborn son of John and Priscilla of early Plymouth days. Much of his time had lately been spent "to the eastward," where he assisted Governor Phips in protecting the Maine villages against the Indians. The girls had picked up some gossip that his relations with the latter were more cordial than were deemed decent. But though they were familiar with his spectral shape, they had yet to meet him in the flesh, and when they were asked to indicate him in court, they pointed to the wrong man.

Alden could be excused a small grin. He had been irritated at the order that he make the inconvenient journey to Salem, and had obeyed only because Deputy Governor Stoughton had issued an express command. It was as he thought; the girls didn't know him from Adam, or anyway from a Captain Hill who stood at his side.

The magistrates, however, were not satisfied. "The light is bad here," said one. "Take him outside and let the girls view him by daylight."

Outside the girls broke into full cry, "Thou art the man!" He was led back to court where he indignantly turned on the magistrates. "Just why do your honors suppose I have no better things to do than to come to Salem to afflict these persons that I never knew or saw before?"

The magistrates ignored this outburst. It was time to begin the touch test. This had become the most important office of the girls, and over the months the method had been reduced to a science. First Alden was commanded to look at the girls. As his evil eye met theirs, they collapsed and writhed on the floor. Then came the second part of the test. His head was averted, his right hand held out, and the hand of each girl guided to meet his. The touch drew the venom back into the witch, and the girl came to her senses, stood and grew silent.

107

It was considered an infallible test, impressive to all beholders. It did not impress Alden, who performed a test on his own. He turned to a friend on the bench and caught his eye.

"Now I look at you," he said. "How is it you don't fall down like these girls?"

His friend was a friend no longer. He had come hoping to help Alden. But to him as to most witnesses in these distracted times, the demonstration had been utterly convincing.

"Confess and give glory to God," he said.

"I hope to give glory to God but not to gratify the devil," retorted Alden. "I wonder at God in suffering these creatures with their juggling tricks to accuse innocent people."

Boston jail being crowded and Alden eminent, he was placed under house arrest. He still had friends; one was Judge Samuel Sewall who came to pray with him. But as the heat of the summer waxed and Alden saw how the trials were going, he placed no dependence on the prayers of a friend who was also a judge. He fled to Duxbury, where a friend kept him in hiding. Duxbury was next to Plymouth, and no one in those parts had succumbed to the witch mania.

Alden made his court appearance late in May, just three days before the arraignment of the first of what was to be a long line of Andover witches.

There had been suspicion of witchcraft there for a long time, and to no one's surprise it had fastened on Martha Carrier, who was the local equivalent of Sarah

Good. She had been "warned out" in 1690 when she arrived with her brood of children, and again when she was accused of spreading smallpox "with wicked carelessness." The warnings had somehow not got rid of her; the charge of witchcraft did.

There was no lack of evidence. Many of her neighbors had quarreled with her, and swore out depositions attesting to the mischief that followed: mysterious pains, ulcers, the reopening and festering of old wounds, the unaccountable death of healthy cows. What is more her children glibly testified that she had also made witches of them. Eight-year-old Sarah said that her mother took the form of a cat.

"How did you know that the cat was your mother?"

"The cat told me so."

The visionary girls of Salem Village furnished other details. The devil had promised to make her queen of hell, Burroughs being the king. She failed to pass the touch test, and made insolent responses to the magistrates who had no compunction about holding her for trial.

But they had barely begun with Andover. One of its most substantial citizens, Joseph Ballard, had long been troubled by the illness of his wife, for which no doctor could find a cause or remedy. That she was a victim of witchcraft seemed obvious, and though he made no charge against Martha Carrier, he hoped that her departure would bring relief.

He hoped in vain. Jailing Martha did not end his wife's suffering, nor did putting the witch in chains.

109

Other witches still undiscovered were manifestly at work, and Ballard was determined to find them. To this end he sent an unusual request to Salem; he asked for the loan of Ann Putnam.

Ann, now the youngest of the circle, had long been its most trusted member. She had never wavered in her testimony; no observer had ever accused her of trickery. Never had she like some of the girls, including Abigail, bragged of her familiarity with the devil. Devoted to her mother, who was pregnant and now seldom able to attend the hearings, she had dedicated her whole soul to exposing the wickedness that threatened Salem Village.

The magistrates could ill spare her, but in July they consented to a brief leave of absence. Ballard sent horse and man to fetch her, and undertook to bear the expense of her visit. Ann, however, rode her father's mare. Shy before strangers, at the last moment she had persuaded Mary Walcott to come with her, and Mary rode the Ballard horse.

The summer's ride down country lanes was a pleasant outing for the girls, but there was one mishap. Just as the spire of Andover meetinghouse came in sight, the Putnam mare shied and sent Ann flying over her head. The child climbed back unhurt and with a revelation. Only a witch could unseat a Putnam, and she and her horse had spotted this one, an Andover witch sending her shape to head off inquiry. The woman was a stranger to Ann, but she had seen her clearly and would know her when she saw her in the flesh.

A tender, indeed a reverent welcome awaited the girls in Andover. Who were they but priestesses appointed by God Himself to ferret out the devil and drive him from the colony? What sacrifices they had made, what pains suffered in performing their holy office!

An honor guard rode out to meet them, and they were escorted to the Ballard doorstep to the sound of fife and drum. A minister stood there to bless their mission with a prayer. He was not the senior pastor, the Reverend Francis Dane, but his young assistant, Thomas Bernard. The girls read no significance into this fact, but the townspeople did. Their venerable pastor did not approve the experiment about to take place. Inwardly, if not yet outwardly, he echoed the indignation of Increase Mather when an ailing child in his parish was taken to Salem for diagnosis by the girls: "Is there no God in Boston that you must send to the devil in Salem?"

The pastor remained in the background and bided his time. Perhaps no harm would come of the visit. In Salem, town and village, he suspected that these girls were guided by local gossip and neighborly malice. Here they were innocent of such knowledge. If they saw witches as expected they could not identify them. Dane had not heard of the touch test.

After so long a journey the girls were not put to work at once. They were given the best chamber and a fine canopied four-poster to rest in. Ann, who was tired, said a brief prayer and stretched out. Mary, who was not, propped herself up with the fat bolsters stuffed with goose down and took up her knitting.

But when they were led to the sickroom to begin their office, it was frail Ann who had the strength. At the very threshold Mary was overcome and collapsed whimpering to the floor. Ann, who had learned to brace herself against the preliminary, less deathly onslaughts of witchcraft, nerved herself to remain upright and fix her eyes on the bed. She saw not one witch but two, one at the head, one at the foot, both tormenting poor Goody Ballard.

"Their names! Their names!" cried Joseph Ballard. "Who are these devils?"

As the pastor had foreseen, Ann did not know. "Tell me your names," she said gently, as if to a child. "Tell me your names that I may know who you are."

Such questioning had not worked since Burroughs. Instead of obliging, the witches came at Ann with such venom that she too cried out and fell.

In other sickrooms the results were no better, even when the girls described how the witches were dressed. "Mark you, that one wears a white hood." There was no lack of white hoods in Andover, or checked aprons, or sad colored skirts that looked as if they had dragged in the mud. Without names the descriptions were no help, and the girls knew no names.

Acquaintance with local gossip would have enlightened them, but they had no such acquaintance. That was partly due to the influence of Francis Dane. He disliked the experiment, but since take place it must, it must be done fairly. It was clear to him that the case against Martha Carrier rested largely on the spite of her

112

neighbors. To the best of his ability he imposed a quarantine on these girls against such spite.

In time means might have been found to get around this prohibition, but time was what Andover did not have. In Salem the trials were continuing; new witches came in daily. The magistrates could not long spare their best witnesses. Something must be done quickly. Andover had no choice but resort to the touch test.

Chief Justice Daniel Bradstreet, son of the former governor, arranged the details. To convince skeptics it must take place publicly, in the meetinghouse. The pastor objected but was overruled, by his assistant, by nearly all his deacons.

A precaution was taken to insure fairness. When the girls were led into the building they would find there not only characters of ill repute, already under suspicion, but matrons of irreproachable conduct, the pastor's own daughter and granddaugher, the wives of the deacons. Some men were included in the lineup.

So it was arranged, and the girls were led in to perform the test. And what happened was a worse catastrophe for Andover than as if an earthquake had brought the steeple and all the timbers crashing down upon those within.

As the girls passed down the aisle and met the eyes of one after another, they fell to the floor in an extremity of agony. Only when the malefactors' hands were guided to theirs did their torments leave them. Their accusations fell like the rain on the just and the unjust, and this in full daylight before the eyes of the assembled villagers.

Husbands saw faithful wives of twenty years demonstrate "diabolical molestation"; sons saw mothers, brothers saw sisters, and to a man they believed the terrible evidence. How could any not believe who had witnessed the cruel suffering of the innocent girls?

Even some of the accused were convinced. One of them, Mary Osgood, wife of a deacon, racked her brain when she was taken to court in Salem to recall when and how she had become a witch.

"It must have been twelve years ago when my last child was born," she decided. "It was a hard birth, and I was long ill and in deep depression. I remember that I was often attended by a cat, but I then no whit suspected the cat to be the devil."

All the accused were, as they reported later, "utterly astonished and amazed and consternated even out of reason." Nevertheless some of them clung to reason and would not confess even when husbands and brothers insisted that they do so.

Forty warrants were signed by Bradstreet before he quit. He himself had arranged this examination; suddenly he no longer believed in it. He paid for his skepticism. The example of Ann and Mary had caused a circle of afflicted girls to rise up in Andover, and they cried out that he and his wife had committed nine spectral murders. He went into hiding, and his brother John, who had bewitched a dog, ran for safety to New Hampshire.

Two Andover men were accused, Samuel Wardwell and William Barker, and both confessed. The former connected his witchcraft with his habit of crying "the devil take it" when he was annoyed. The latter had been tempted by the devil's promise that under his rule all men should be equal and "live bravely." He also offered a witch census: there were 307 in Essex County alone.

The panic in Andover was extreme, but it quickly ran its course. The justice of the peace was the first to come to his senses. Then husbands repented that they had "broken charity" with their wives and petitioned to get them back. In jail Wardwell met the sane and resolute John Procter and under his influence recanted his confession.

Andover was a turning point. The delusion had not ended in Massachusetts, but the end was near. It was not long after Ann returned from her outing that she fell prey to her first doubt.

12

Mary Warren had rightly suspected that the unstable temper of her mistress Betty Procter was due to the stress of early pregnancy. By August 5 when the Procters came to trial, there was no doubt about her condition. She escaped sentencing by, as the blunt Puritan phrase put it, "pleading her belly."

But if the judges would not hang the mother of a child still unborn, they had no such compunction about its father. John Procter was condemned to take his turn at the scaffold on Gallows Hill on August 19.

He pleaded hard for a postponement. Was that cowardice? If so, not that alone. Procter had got into the witchcraft by attacking the logic on which the hunt was being conducted. From prison he had continued the attack. He had renewed his petition to the Boston ministers to investigate the means by which confessions were wrung from male prisoners. If Martha Carrier's eight-year-old daughter had glibly acknowledged her mother's sorceries, her older sons had done so only after being chained head to heels until the blood came.

Procter's own elder son had undergone a similar ordeal, but without confessing. Now he had a promise that the investigation would be conducted; some ministers were already interviewing prisoners in Boston, but their conclusions had not yet been published. A stay of execution was needed to give them time.

Even more important, one of Procter's friends, who had circulated the petition among his former neighbors in Ipswich, was boldly challenging the whole groundwork of the trials, the use of spectral evidence. The judges held that God would not permit the shape of the innocent to appear before the afflicted. John Wise, the Ipswich pastor, was calling attention to the fact that God had given such permission in the case of Job. He had not only permitted Satan, he had positively invited him to do his worst against a man of irreproachable character. And when all Job's friends deserted him, convinced that he could not suffer guiltless, God had not.

Let the judges listen to such reasoning, let them discard the hallucinations of a pack of crazed girls, and what was left of the case against John Procter and his fellow prisoners?

But the judges were not ready to listen, and on August 19 Procter and four others were loaded into a cart and trundled up a hill in Salem where the hangman waited. Procter looked about him and wondered how it went with the fields he had been plowing and planting when this insanity began. His own fields, close to the Topsfield line, he could not see. What he did see everywhere was neglect. The witchcraft had dislocated normal life. Few farmers could pay proper attention to their land and beasts while the terror had them by the throat. Some had fled, leaving the crows and weeds to take over what had come up of their planting.

A crowd more numerous than ordinary waited on Gallows Hill. They had not been drawn by the fate of John Procter, best known only to his neighbors, or even Martha Carrier, queen of hell, who also rode in the cart. They had come to watch justice done on the most notorious criminal of all, the faithless minister, George Burroughs.

They had come even from Boston in the person of young Cotton Mather. His father Increase had attended the trial and reported, "Had I been one of the judges I could not have acquitted him." Cotton had come to witness the outcome. If he had not, the hanging might not have taken place.

At the foot of the gallows each person, male or female, was given an opportunity to pray. Burroughs made his long and eloquent, and at its conclusion, faultlessly, not missing a syllable, he repeated the Lord's Prayer.

When he turned to the scaffold the crowd surged forward. Was not this the supreme proof of innocence, the repetition of the Lord's Prayer? But for the quick action of Mather they might have snatched him from the hangman. But Mather swung himself into the saddle of his white horse and spoke.

"The devil is never more the devil," he told them, "than when he most appears like an angel of light."

The crowd had heard such reasoning before. Lawson

118

had spoken thus of both Martha Cory and Rebecca Nurse. It was a cliché of the witchcraft and for this reason effective. The crowd halted and let the hangman do his work.

From somewhere in the crowd the voice of Mercy Lewis shrilled out. "He did not speak of himself. The black man whispered the words in his ear."

At her side Ann Putnam turned and stared.

"How do you know?"

"I saw."

Ann was bewildered. How was it that Mercy had seen what she had not? It had never happened before except in strictly private experience, like Mercy's report of being taken by Burroughs to a mountaintop to look on the kingdoms of the world. Since that had happened in Mercy's childhood and to her alone, Ann naturally could not know of it. But this was public. Never before on such occasion had Mercy seen what Ann had missed. She, not Mercy, was a "visionary girl."

Her reflections were interrupted by the grim events on the gallows, but on the ride home her puzzlement returned and she questioned Mercy.

"Are you sure? Was the black man really doing that?"

"Am I a liar?"

"The devil is. The devil may have tricked you. The devil cannot repeat holy words."

"I heard him!" cried Mercy.

Ann fell silent, but she was troubled. She would have liked to confide in someone older and wiser than she. Her mother? No, she could not trouble her ailing mother, now as far gone in pregnancy as Betty Procter. Her father? She didn't know how to bring up the subject. Her pastor? No child, not even his own daughter, had ever confided in the Reverend Samuel Parris. The community, however steadfast in the prosecution of the witchcraft, was growing away from him. Ann could only dismiss the subject from her mind, or try. And now she kept when she could away from Mercy; she no longer trusted the Putnam handmaid.

A month later she was strangely though differently troubled by the death of Giles Cory. It did not take place on the scaffold, for Giles had not been condemned or even found guilty. He refused to plead at all. He stood mute.

When Martha had been accused months back he had testified against her, at least that was what he seemed to be doing. Compared to the testimony of the girls, who had visibly undergone agonies at Martha's hands and had seen her as a yellow bird hopping from beam to beam of the meetinghouse, what Giles reported did not amount to much. All he could say was that he had been bothered by his wife's fluency in prayer. A recent professor of the faith and at best inarticulate, he found it difficult to pray at all when Martha was with him. Sometimes he gave up and went to bed, leaving her on her knees before the fireplace.

The only significance that the magistrates could read into this was that Ann Putnam had caught Martha praying to the devil. That being so, no wonder her old husband was troubled. Only once at Martha's examination had Giles been roused to passionate utterance. It was when he was asked if the strange appearance of a beast had frightened him.

"I do not know that I ever used that word in my life!" he flared.

Nor would he take fright when he himself was accused and brought to trial. Martha was then still living in Boston jail, but she had been tried and condemned to hang. Already her congregation had pronounced the sentence of excommunication upon her. It had been done *in absentia* because Parris had such experience of her sharp tongue when he visited her in prison that he would not risk a public ceremony.

And now Giles knew that however her prayers had confused him, his Martha was no witch. Turning the matter in his slow mind, he had long suspected it; when the same charge was made against him on the same sort of evidence, he was certain. Before the trial could take place he made plans. He revised his will, cutting from it those of his children by a former marriage who had testified against Martha, and deeding everything to those who had not done so. Then, knowing that the property of a condemned witch or wizard went not to the heirs but to the authorities, he resolved not to stand trial at all. What use to plead innocence? The girls would only make a mockery of him as they had of Martha. So when he was taken before the judges he stood mute.

English law provided a remedy against such obstinacy, "la peine forte et dure." The prisoner was laid on his back and heavy weights placed on his chest. The object was not to kill, but to force the accused to speak. Giles did speak once. When death delayed interminably, he cried, "More weight!" It was applied and at last he died.

The ordeal went on for hours, all of a long Monday, and stirred people as even the hangings had not. Some gathered around to watch and marvel that so old a man could endure so much. Young Ann was among the watchers, but at a distance. She lay at home on her bed, fighting for breath against a suffocating weight. Why did the fate of Giles so afflict a child who had watched most of the hangings? Perhaps it was only that it went on so long. A hanging, however painful, was soon over, and brought relief to the victims of the condemned. This punishment went on and on, and the innocent child suffered with the guilty old man.

At last the child caught a full breath and looked up in wonder. It happened at the exact moment of Giles's death, or so the Putnams reckoned. A spirit had come to Ann with a story so remarkable that her father made a record of it and hurried it to the magistrates.

Years ago, long before Ann was born, one of Giles's hired men had died under mysterious circumstances, with "cloddens of blood about his heart." Unpopular with his neighbors, with whom he was often involved in lawsuits, hot-tempered Giles was brought to court on the charge of beating the man to death. A jury, however, found the death due to natural causes, and Giles was let off.

Now a spirit in a winding-sheet visited Ann to report the truth. He was the hired man, and he had indeed been murdered by Giles. He reported that when his

122

murderer made his compact with the evil one, the devil had promised that he would never hang. God had hardened Giles's heart against giving testimony and so suffer an easier death. "It must be done to him as it was to me," the ghost told Ann.

Her father rushed the girl's statement to the judges, and Samuel Sewall for one was much relieved to hear it, for the fate of Giles had been hard to take. Putnam could not stop discussing his wonder at the revelation.

"That happened before the child was born," he said, and counted on his fingers. "Why it was all of five years before. Without her spectral sight she could have known nothing of it."

"And was it never spoken of before her?" asked his half brother.

The conversation took place in Ingersoll's ordinary. Joseph now avoided the household of his half brother like the plague, but he had run into Thomas here. The latter turned his back on him without reply. Neither did Ann, who was here today, reply, but she had heard.

Another vision came to her: herself as a young child sitting by the fire, listening to neighbors who had dropped in for a winter evening's gossip. She heard their voices. They were talking about Giles, about that ancient charge of murder, some defending, some denouncing. The whole scene played out before her, and she stared at it bewildered. Where did truth lie, in this memory or in the vision of the man in the winding-sheet? Her own words rang suddenly in her ears: "The devil is a liar. The devil may have tricked you."

"Father!" she called, then choked and fell to the floor.

"You doubt my poor child, you dare doubt her!" cried Thomas. "Look at this."

"Take her home," said Joseph. "She deserves better than what she gets from you."

There was kindness in his voice. Ann opened her eyes and looked at him. Was he one in whom she could confide? But another memory long suppressed rose up, something Uncle Joseph had said about a woman in Springfield hanged for raising the spirit of her dead child. Ann screamed and fell in a fit so sore that there was nothing for it but to take her home.

13

Ann recovered, but she now seemed a different person. When her father next prepared to take her to court, she didn't want to go.

"It's your duty, child," Putnam said. "We are in a way to clear all Massachusetts of its witches. The judges need you."

"My mother needs me too," said Ann. "Let Mercy go."

Putnam did not care to say that Mercy no longer found favor with the judges. It was not that they suspected her of trickery, but they had taken a dislike to her manner. In court, unless actively involved in a fit, she cast wanton eyes on the younger men. During recess she often went out with one man or another. Once when she and her fellow were about to disappear into a hayloft, she turned on Ann.

"You're not to tell," she said. "Don't you tell no one where we be."

Ann obeyed but in surprise. She was not an ignorant child. The birth of babies, brought forth in sorrow according to the curse of Eve, she had witnessed down to the grimmest detail on the "groaning stool." She knew, though somewhat less explicitly, how babies were conceived. Where her ignorance lay was in the nature of fleshly temptation. In that she was a child still, and a child she would all her life remain. The experiences she was undergoing lay like a chill on her, arresting her growth as a frost arrests a bud put forth too early. The blooming of womanhood was not for this little Puritan nun.

"Let me stay with Mother," she pleaded.

"Mercy shall stay," said her father. "They can do without Mercy."

Ann said strangely, apropos of nothing, "That minister prayed. He said the Lord's Prayer."

She spoke so softly that her father may not have heard. If he did he found no sense in the remark. "Come," he said, and Ann obeyed, and when in court the rest of the sisterhood cried out, she cried too and fell and writhed. But the judges found her testimony less valuable than it had been before. Her vision was clouded.

When the time came for more hangings — one of which included Martha Cory — Ann managed to stay behind on the plea of illness. Her father wanted her present. Most Puritan parents wanted their children to view a hanging. There was high moral edification in witnessing the fate of a criminal who would not repent his crimes. But Ann remained with her mother, and so missed hearing the "eminent prayer" which Martha was allowed to make at the foot of the scaffold. Did she too

126

repeat Holy Writ? If so Ann was happier that she could not hear her.

The hangings Ann missed took place on September 9 and 22. The first included seven women; besides Martha Cory, Rebecca Nurse's youngest sister Mary Esty was among them. Of her Ann was presently to hear a rare report.

The hanging of September 22 was the most numerous of all, "eight firebrands of hell," as the Reverend Nicholas Noyes of Salem sorrowfully put it. Samuel Wardwell of Andover was the only man among the condemned, originally a confessor he had at the cost of his life renounced his confession. At the foot of the gallows he tried to present his reasons to the people of Salem, but failed because smoke from the sheriff's pipe blew into his face and choked him. According to the girls the devil had blown the smoke.

It was the last of the witchcraft hangings, though no one knew it then. Every jail in Essex County, to say nothing of Boston and Charlestown, was crowded beyond capacity, and some of the inmates had already been condemned, yet there would be no more hangings. A strange pause had come in the prosecution, ill understood by the girls on whom it had depended.

The protests against the method by which the trials had been conducted were finally taking effect. Husbands in Andover urgently pleaded for the return of their wives. Increase Mather had at last investigated the means by which confessions were obtained and was ill pleased by what he learned. The judges themselves were embarrassed at the number of times they had to tell one girl or another that her accusation was mistaken.

Judge Saltonstall had been accused shortly after he left the bench in indignation at the way the case of Rebecca Nurse was handled. So was the kinswoman of a Boston minister who had denounced the use of spectral evidence. So was Lady Phips, wife of the governor, who during his absence to quell Indian uprisings "to the eastward," had signed the release of a prisoner personally known to her.

Phips himself returned to Boston to find himself faced with a fury of public protest. It was not that God-fearing people had ceased to believe in the reality of witchcraft, but a great many had come to believe that this was no way to combat it. Phips put a stop to the trials until the magistrates and ministers could find a more rational basis to continue them.

The girls were not consulted in these deliberations. They only knew that their services were less in demand than they had been. However, early in October, while the trials were still in abeyance they were invited to Gloucester to uncover its witches.

That witchcraft was at work there had been known for some time. During July, garrison outposts had been besieged by creatures wearing blue shirts, who by the blackness of their hair had been taken for Indians or Frenchmen, or both. When bullets had no effect on them, the garrisons realized that the invasion was spectral. The girls were called on to solve the mystery, and now that they had leisure they came, accompanied by a Gloucester constable.

Their way took them across the Ipswich River. The bridge was narrow and shaky; for safety's sake the girls picked their way across on foot, leading their horses. At the Ipswich end they fell all of a heap with clamorous outcry. They had met a witch.

Their shrieks drew a crowd, but it behaved like no other crowd they knew. "She's a witch!" they cried. "Arrest that witch who torments us before she kills us quite."

Nothing happened. The old woman was let alone, though the girls howled until the froth came to their mouths. People looked down at them as at the tumbling of animals. This was Ipswich, not Salem, and Ipswich had not bid them here. These were people who had signed a petition testifying to their faith in the innocence of John Procter, and these were the girls who had done that good man to death.

"Who brought these wenches here?" one man asked, and then turned to the constable. "Then get them on their nags and on their way. We have no use for their kind."

Ann had fallen and cried out with the rest; now she found difficulty in getting up.

"Take me home," she gasped. "I'm ill. I can go no further."

The constable had no mind to double back on his journey, nor could he send Ann alone, unless she walked, for she and Mercy rode one horse, and Mercy would not give up her mount. The constable appealed to the onlookers.

"Will no one for charity's sake care for this child

until we return?" He looked into stony faces. Giving shelter to one responsible for the death of John Procter was beyond the call of charity. He lifted Ann to her horse, but she was hardly able to sit there. Gloucester was too far a ride for her. Then he thought of a minister in Beverly whose charity never failed. It meant a wide detour, but he got her at last to the door of the Reverend John Hale.

For a bad moment it looked as if there would be no welcome even there. The pastor was afield, and when his lady heard who these girls were she shrank back.

"Which one asks to stay?" she asked, and exclaimed at the reply. "Ann Putnam! Ann *Put*nam?"

Wherever Ann went among strangers, she heard an awed whisper, "That one is Ann Putnam." But she had never heard this tone before. Trembling she went forward.

"The barn is all I ask. If I could rest there . . ."

Mrs. Hale stared. She had never seen "the visionary maid," but her reputation was ten foot tall.

"Why it's only a little girl!" she cried. "Child, come in."

"The stable will do," gasped Ann, but Mrs. Hale led her into the house. "When do you return?" she asked over her shoulder. The constable didn't know.

The Hale home was more modest than that of the Ballards in Andover, but the featherbed on which Ann was placed was as comfortable. She lay on it all afternoon, rousing only when a maidservant brought her a bowl of soup. Where she was or why she no longer knew

130

or cared. All that mattered was the sense of loving kindness that enfolded her like the eiderdown quilt her hostess had spread over her.

At early dusk Mrs. Hale came to her.

"Are you well enough to come down? The pastor is home now. We'll have family prayers and then we'll sup."

Ann came down and made a curtsey to the pastor, who looked at her keenly, but with kindness. She bowed her head while he prayed and read from the Bible.

No part of Holy Writ was unfamiliar to Ann, but the pastor's choice was less familiar than most. When her father performed what were called "family duties," he most often turned to her mother's favorite, the book of Revelation. How often had Ann trembled to hear of the whore of Babylon, of the saints who had blood to drink, and of the bottomless pit from which rose the beast "that was and is not and yet is." There was comfort in that book too, "God shall wipe all tears from their eyes," but Ann best remembered the terror.

This pastor read from the Book of Job, that just and upright man whom God had permitted Satan to afflict with sore temptation. And Job, though condemned by all his friends, stood steadfast. "What," he had said to his bitter wife, "shall we receive good at the hand of God and shall we not receive evil?"

At these words, which rang strangely in her ears, Ann lifted her head and met the eyes of the pastor, who suddenly closed his book.

"Are you well now?" he asked. "Are you rested

enough from your journey to do my bidding?" Ann nodded. "What I ask is very simple. Look into the eyes of my wife."

Ann turned to Mrs. Hale, who flinched from her gaze until her husband grasped her hand. Their eyes met steadily then, and Ann's were the first to fall.

"Are you well?" repeated the pastor gently. "Is it still well with you?"

"I am well," said Ann. What did these people want of her? Mrs. Hale rose to the occasion.

"How can it be well with her when she's hungry? We'll sup now."

"And after," said the pastor, his eyes on Ann, "I have a tale to tell. Do you remember Mary Esty?"

"None of that!" said his wife. She who had been timid before, reluctant to meet Ann's eyes, was now in command. "Would you have the child die of hunger?"

They ate in silence and Ann turned her mind to Mary Esty. She was one of Rebecca Nurse's younger sisters, still in her fifties, without the frailty of Rebecca or the hot temper of Sarah Cloyce. Ann more than remembered. She saw Goody Esty as clearly as she had one day in court. What impressed her now was the kindness in her eyes. Why, when she had longed for someone in whom to confide her bewilderment over the fate of George Burroughs, here was one who would have understood. But then Mary lay in jail under sentence of death, and now it had been carried out.

At the examination her collected and gentle manner had impressed the magistrates. "Are you certain this is the woman?" they asked the girls. The implied doubt sent them into convulsions, writhing and screaming. Only Ann found the breath to answer. Again she heard her voice shrill out.

"Oh Goody Esty, you are the woman! You are the woman!"

Had she thus cried out now before the Hales? Ann knew only that they were looking at her strangely.

"What think you of this?" a magistrate had then asked Mary.

"It is an evil spirit, but whether it be witchcraft I cannot tell."

After she was sent to prison the magistrates still had doubts, especially when the jailers reported that they found no fault in her. They undertook a test which they performed too seldom. They called in the girls for questioning one by one. Ignorant as they were of the nature of hysteria, they were well aware that the girls in concert caught their fits from each other as by contagion. So they consulted them singly and found them no longer sure. Even Ann, so positive in court, thought she might have been in error.

And Mary, giving glory to God for her release, went home. She remained there just three days. The one girl who had not absolved her, Mercy Lewis, went into such convulsions that the Putnams all but gave her up for dead. Her jaws locked so that she could not name her tormentor, though sometimes she gasped out a prayer.

"Dear Lord, receive my soul. Lord, let her not kill me quite."

The magistrates were troubled that they had accepted the word of the other girls against this one. They called on the others to name the tormentor. It was indeed Mary Esty. Ann saw her, and Mary Walcott saw the nature of the torment — chains had been drawn tight about Mercy's throat — and the reason. The witch had managed to blind all the girls except this one; she had to kill her.

Mary returned to jail, but after condemnation she sent a petition to the judges "not for my own life, for I know I must die and my appointed time is set, but that no more innocent blood be shed, which undoubtedly cannot be avoided in the way and course you go in. I question not but your honors do to the utmost of your pains in the discovery and detection of witchcraft and witches, and would not be guilty of innocent blood for the world, but by my own innocency I know you are in the wrong way."

She pleaded for a more careful examination of the confessing witches, "I being confident there are several of them have belied themselves and others. . . . They say myself and others have made a league against the devil. I know and the Lord he knows they belie me, and so I question not that they do others; and the Lord alone who is the searcher of hearts knows that . . . I know not the least thing of witchcraft; therefore I cannot, I durst not belie my soul."

When the meal was done Ann was alone with the Hales. The little servingmaid who attended them had been given leave to visit a friend in the neighborhood. The pastor filled his pipe from a jar on the mantle,

134

settled himself in his chair, and then told Ann that he had a strange and troubling tale to tell.

"There is a maid of Wenham who has lately been afflicted. Mary Herrick. Do you know the girl?"

Ann did not. Wenham was out of her way, nor could she recall that any from that village had ever been present in court. "Are there witches there?" she asked "I didn't know."

"There are none. Nor was it a woman of Wenham Mary saw in her affliction. It was Mary Esty."

"But they hanged her!" cried Ann. She was stunned. No witch had ever returned from the grave to afflict. If God permitted it, of what service were the hangings?

"Mary Herrick first saw her before she hanged. The shape of Mary Esty came to this girl and said, 'I am going on the ladder to be hanged, but I am innocent, and before a twelfth month is past you shall believe it."

"Being alive, she could come then," said Ann, "though I never heard of such a thing. How did she afflict?"

"She only spoke and did nothing. The affliction came after."

"The girl lied! No witch has ever risen from the grave."

"No lie," said Hale. "The girl may have been deranged, though she never was before, but she does not lie. She went to her pastor and he brought her to me to hear her testimony. But you are right. No witch from the grave afflicted her. Mary Esty came again, but only watched, her hands at her side while the girl suffered. It was another who afflicted."

"Another? It was a living witch?"

"It was not. The woman she saw is beyond reproach. Yet the pair came often. It was the same scene. Mary Esty stood silent, her hands at her side, while the other pulled and pinched. At last the afflicter spoke. 'Do you think I am a witch?' she asked. 'No!' cried the Wenham maid, 'You be the devil!' Then her tormentor vanished and came no more. Mary alone remained. Smiling she spoke to the maid, 'Be not afraid but go to your pastor and go to Mr. Hale and tell what you have seen.' That is my tale. What think you of it?"

"God does not permit the devil to take the shape of the innocent. It's in Holy Writ."

"Can you name the text?"

Ann tried to reply but her mouth writhed soundlessly. Her eyes widened and fixed on the invisible world. The Hales looked on in consternation at the beginning of possession. Then Ann cried out to Mrs. Hale.

"It was you! You are that woman she saw!"

Hale was appalled. "It's not for nothing that they call her the visionary maid," he murmured. "I did wrong to tell her."

But his wife who had trembled before was no longer fearful. She took Ann's hand in a warm grasp and managed to fix her tranced eyes on her own.

"Did I afflict thee?" she asked. Unconsciously she fell into the formal language of the court. Ann screamed wildly.

"No! No! You did not. And if I cried out on you in my fits I knew not what I did."

"You did no harm, dear child." Then Mrs. Hale added thoughtfully, "Not to me."

"But I said it to Mary Esty. I said 'You are the woman.' I said that." Ann was sobbing beyond control.

"We'll put you to bed," said Mrs. Hale, and did so. Returning she asked her husband, "What is the meaning of this strange Providence?"

"God has sent us a parable from the grave to chide us for accepting spectral evidence. There has never been truth in it. This child is sick and needs her mother. We won't wait for the constable to return. I'll fetch her home tomorrow."

"And will you tell this tale to her pastor?"

Hale shook his head. He knew Parris too well and had long deplored his way of disregarding a lifetime of good works at the first word of accusation. It crossed his mind to wonder what he would have done if Mrs. Parris had been the afflicter of the vision. He wouldn't put it past him to have her before the magistrates next morning.

"There's no need. The trials have stopped. When they go on I think we'll hear no more of spectral evidence."

14

If Ann needed her mother, her mother had even more need of her. When Hale brought the child to her home late the next morning, her father, red-eyed and distraught, paced the kitchen, trying not to hear the moaning from the chamber that led off it.

"Ann, thank God you've come!" said Putnam. "How could my man fetch you from Gloucester so soon?"

Ann did not hear him. Her eyes were on the chamber where her mother writhed on her bed under the hands of two midwives.

"How long?" she whispered.

"Since dusk last night. It goes hard with her. The midwives say it is a witch who prevents her from giving birth. Go to her, Ann, and see what deviltry this is."

The voice of Hale, whom he had not seen, broke in harshly.

"Leave the devil be, Thomas. It is God who laid this burden on women. Let us go to Him in prayer."

Putnam was hardly capable of taking in Hale's words,

but he bowed his head. It was a strange prayer; only Ann understood it.

"Oh God, forgive us all. We have forgotten what our fathers came into the wilderness to see. The fury of the storm raised by Satan hath fallen heavily upon us. We who walked in clouds could not see our way. God be merciful to us all, and help this woman in her hour of sore need. Turn her sorrow into joy."

Having spoken, the minister was gone without waiting to enjoy the hospitality of the hearth. Like most men he stood in awe of the mystery, sacred and profane, which only women know. Even good Dr. Griggs had seldom looked on the nakedness of birth.

Ann went to the chamber and grasped her mother's hot hand. "I am here, Mother. We have had prayers and God will help you."

Her mother had come into a remission of her pains. She lifted her daughter's hand to her forehead and tried to smile.

"Help me, Ann. I need a sign from God. Go to the Bible, thrust your hand into the book of Revelation, and read me what it lights on. It will be God's sign to me."

The child hesitated. She had often heard Parris denounce this practice as a kind of fortune-telling. Yet she could not deny her mother.

At the great family Bible she hesitated again. Must it be Revelation? What if her hand fell upon the passage about the woman clothed in the sun travailing to give birth, and the great red dragon waiting to devour her child?

"Ann, quickly!" cried her mother.

Ann opened the Bible and read. "And I saw a new heaven and a new earth, for the first heaven and the first earth were passed away."

"And will no more be brought to mind," gasped her mother. "It is a blessed word."

The child stared into the text. Where had her mother found words that were not in this verse? She read on, "And God shall wipe every tear from their eyes, and death shall be no more. Neither shall there be mourning nor crying nor pains any more . . ."

She was interrupted by a great cry. Her father covered his ears and wept, but the child stood listening. She knew that cry, the last before deliverance. And then she heard another, the bawling of the child drawing its first convulsive breath.

The midwives exclaimed at the size and weight of the infant. Never had they delivered a babe so large and at birth so hearty.

"Come see your sister, your daughter," one called. "It's an infant giant."

Putnam's only thought was for his wife. He rushed to her and would have clasped her in his arms had not a midwife shoved him away.

"Leave her be. The woman has labored hard and needs rest not lovemaking."

The younger Ann fetched warm water in a basin and watched the midwives do what was needful for mother and child. Her mother had sunk back on her pillows; once her eyes flickered open to catch a shy smile from her child.

"It's over, Mother," whispered the girl. "And never was such a handsome baby."

The birth was a turning point. The child was lusty, demanding of her rightful needs but unfretful otherwise. After a few days the mother got back her strength. Gone were the nightmares which had haunted her so many years and had become an obsession during her pregnancy. The text from Revelation had become a faithful prophecy for the Putnam household: a new heaven and a new earth.

The old was brought to mind when Mercy Lewis returned from Gloucester in a fit of sulks. The girls had not been received there with the homage to which they were used. They had been summoned by a minority of believers who could not prevent skeptics from pushing into their seances and making rude remarks about the veracity of the girls. Some of the latter were distracted out of their fits and saw no witches. Mercy was of sterner stuff. She shrieked, frothed at the mouth, rolled on the floor, and rose to point her finger at a stout matron.

The accusation brought a roar of laughter from the impious and dismay to the faithful. The matron was the respected wife of a local magistrate. After anxious deliberation as to whether Mercy's word could be accepted against the silence of her companions ("She has blinded them," explained Mercy), they gave up and sent the girls packing.

So Mercy returned in sulks and indisposed for duties redoubled by the recent birth. While the elder Ann lay in bed, she required attention; her gigantic babe required even more, and made imperious demands. Mercy was in no mood to comply. She ignored calls and cries, and when ordered to attend them, went on laggard feet.

Once when the younger Ann was in the barn gathering eggs, her father entered the kitchen to find Mercy in a trance, staring into space, oblivious to the howling of the babe and the feeble calls of the mother. Putnam slapped her.

Mercy turned on him with wild eyes. "Do you see her?" she cried. "Why there she stands! She has come to kill . . ."

She got no farther for Putnam slapped her again. Then he was uneasy at what he had done. He recalled John Procter's remedy for bringing his jade Mary Warren out of her fits, and Procter had been hanged. When his daughter came with her basket of eggs, he found an errand to get Mercy out of the way, and asked her who afflicted the howling baby.

"She's wet. She wants changing," said the girl.

"Is that all? Is there none afflicting her? Look sharply, child."

Ann gave her father a frightened glance and then stared at the babe. A vision did rise before her: George Burroughs at the foot of the scaffold flawlessly repeating holy words that no demon could pronounce. Then she saw the gentle face of Mrs. Hale and heard her ask, "When did I afflict thee?"

142

"Let me change it," she said, and when she was done the baby was afflicted no more.

Putnam did not repeat his request. Ann had not answered his question, but plainly she had not seen what Mercy had. Could he trust that wench? Ann was now free of her fits. Were Mercy's no more than an excuse for getting out of work? And what of the eyes she cast at young men. Was she decent company for his young daughters?

He was still in this mood some days later when he learned that a family about to move "to the eastward" was in need of a servingmaid. He surrendered Mercy to them, and Mercy was glad to go. Now that the trials were suspended, life had grown dull. She had once lived in Maine with the Burroughs family and was happy to adventure there again.

Life in the Putnam household was better without her. There was perhaps more work to do, but given the frequency of Mercy's fits, not much more. One could in any case make do without her. When the elder Ann left her bed she was in better health than she had ever been. Her namesake was free of her fits, and the younger girls, who had never been afflicted at all, were good and willing workers at small tasks.

"A new heaven and a new earth," the younger Ann said to herself. "And the old shall no more be brought to mind." She had found the second part of that text in Isaiah, her mother's favorite after Revelation. It was a great consolation, but in this situation it did not long apply.

143

15

The trials could not be suspended forever. Something had to be done about the accused, one hundred and fifty of them, who crowded every jail in eastern Massachusetts to the point of bursting. Given the suffocating misery of their condition, some were likely to die without standing trial, as had long ago happened to Sarah Osburne. Sarah Good's five-year-old Dorcas, once a lively and hearty child, was now a hunted creature in a state not far from idiocy. Andover husbands were importunately petitioning for the release of their wives.

But without trials nothing could be done. Such was the only way to clear the jails; those found guilty could then be hanged, and the innocent released on payment of their jail fees.

Early in January when the trials were resumed, Putnam bade his daughter prepare to ride with him to Salem. The girl was stricken. She had been well so long. Must the old torments begin again? Her father would not listen to her protest.

144

"It is hard, but you must do your duty," he said. "The judges cannot do without your witness."

In that he was misinformed. The judges were ready to do without Ann and the whole circle of the afflicted. Their decision was not unanimous. Chief Justice Stoughton had some misgivings about the restrictions they were about to place on the rules of evidence. Nevertheless after months of discussion, after pressures from Governor Phips, after consultation not only with the ministry of Massachusetts but the Dutch divines of New York, the majority of the magistrates now agreed with Mary Esty that in the conduct of the earlier trials they had been "in the wrong way."

Quivering with fear, fighting for control against rising hysteria, Ann let herself be led to the door of the Salem meetinghouse, but she did not pass through it. John Hale stood there to bar the way and spoke harshly to her father.

"Thomas, why did you bring her? Take the child home to her mother."

"Surely she is needed. How can the judges convict without her testimony?"

"They will listen no more to distracted children. It is agreed that the afflicted are in the worst position to give testimony."

"They take my daughter for a liar?"

"A liar, no." Hale's tone had softened as he looked down at the pale and tremulous Ann; he put a gentle hand on her shoulder. "But the *devil* is a liar and the children could only report the devil's delusions."

For all his respect for the cloth Putnam could not believe him. He caught at the sleeve of Jonathan Corwin, who was passing on his way to court.

"Sir, I brought my daughter to testify. Is it true that the judges will not hear her?"

Ann whispered, "I have nothing to say." Corwin looked down at her intently.

"We go by new rules of evidence. We heard the testimony of the afflicted at the examination. We have no need of them now."

Putnam could not credit even the magistrate. Surely as the trials proceeded, Ann would be sent for. At Hale's suggestion he took her to wait in the ordinary. Others of the circle of the afflicted were already there. Ann avoided them and sat aside with downcast eyes.

Hale had come with them. "What are these new rules?" Putnam asked him.

"The principal thing is that they will no longer accept spectral evidence. It will not be enough to testify that the shape, the spirit of the accused has been doing evil deeds. The bodily presence must be proved. To do otherwise is to condemn on dreams and hallucinations. What defense have I if I can be convicted on what your daughter saw in a dream?"

He should not have made so personal an application. Putnam became almost apoplectic with fury.

"What of the witches my daughter saw drinking blood in the parson's pasture? What of those she saw celebrating unholy rites on the very lawn of our meetinghouse?"

"Did you see them also? Were they there in their bodily presence?"

"It was not given me to see such things."

"Then the evidence was spectral. All the confessing witches saw such things too, and I am told that now many are coming off their confessions. They at least were liars."

Ann had mastered her trembling. Timidly she looked up at Hale, but her eyes were steady as they were grave.

"Sir, did we condemn the innocent?"

"God grant that we did not," said the pastor heavily. "If we did, may God forgive us."

He ordered a mug of cider for the child, and returned to the court where the trials were about to begin. Putnam went with him.

Left to herself Ann brought her mug to a far corner, away from the afflicted sisterhood. One girl, Elizabeth Booth, was on the verge of a convulsion, her limbs jerking strangely. Her anxious mother called to Ann.

"Child, who does this to her? Can you see?"

Ann kept her eye on her mug. "I see nothing."

"But Ann, look at her. A witch is tormenting her and she cannot speak. Look at her, dear child, only look."

Ann was afraid. She had old experience of the contagiousness of fits. She would not rise from her place, but cast a quick glance and said again, "There is nothing to see."

"Has the devil blinded you or is this willful?" demanded the mother.

Ann wished Hale would return to protect her from the woman's wrath. The very thought of the minister heartened her. She began to pray. "Dear God, preserve

147

me. Dear God, keep me from the devil's delusion. Dear God . . ."

She remained in prayer all morning and the prayer kept her steady. Perhaps it helped Elizabeth too, for as men came in from court to report what was going on there and no more attention was paid her, she came to herself and asked for a mug of beer. At noon recess the ordinary was thronged and clamorous with comment on the conduct of judges and their jury.

"God help us, they're in a way to clear them all!"

"God be thanked!"

"God indeed! This be the devil's doing. God will not forgive this wicked smothering of the witchcraft. His hand will lie heavy on Salem."

Putnam came too and brusquely signaled Ann. "Come, girl, they don't want us. We'll go home." He mounted his horse at the hitching post, and Ann climbed to the pillion. She dared not question her father, and he did not speak until they reached home and the younger children ran out with gleeful greeting.

"Did you catch the witches? How many witches did you catch today?"

Putnam angrily brushed them off, left his mare and went in to his wife.

"The judges are possessed!" he exclaimed. "God help us, they're clearing them all. We were in a way to rid all Massachusetts of its witches, and now the judges will let them loose. God be merciful to this country."

Ann timidly touched his sleeve. "Shall I unsaddle the mare?" she asked.

148

Her father glared at her.

"There are ministers worse than these judges. Your friend Mr. Hale is no better than a Sadducee and there is talk about him. I heard a strange tale about his wife."

"Did he not once defend Bridget Bishop, the worst of them all?" asked the elder Ann. "What is this tale?"

Her daughter would not stay to listen. She unsaddled the mare, and finding bread and cheese forgotten in the saddlebags, remained in the stable to nibble at them. In January it was a cold place to lunch, but Ann warmed herself against the flanks of her kind friend the mare.

Not having followed the trials to the end, Putnam was inaccurate in saying that the judges were clearing all the accused. It was true that, denied spectral evidence, they could find no case against those who pleaded their innocence. But when next day and the day after they came to the confessing witches, there was some difference. Most of these, as Hale had said, came off their confessions, admitted that under terror they had lied.

Three did not. The wife of Samuel Wardwell had seen what happened to her husband when he renounced his confession; he had been hanged. For dear life she clung to hers. So did Mary Post, called "senseless and ignorant." So did Elizabeth Johnson, a girl her grandfather, Andover's Reverend Francis Dane, called "simplish at best." The judges had no compunction about these; they condemned them to the gallows.

Yet they did not hang. Neither did five already condemned before the suspension of the trials, but temporarily spared for one cause or another. Governor Phips

149

looked into these cases, the confessors and those condemned earlier, and could find no difference in the evidence brought against them from the evidence brought against those found not guilty. Bred to a rough life on the Maine frontier, he had no legal training at all, but common sense he did have, and by its light he reprieved all the condemned.

One of these was Elizabeth Procter, who had been allowed to live until she could give birth to John's child. In the spring, when the governor proclaimed a general jail delivery, she was released, carrying the child in her arms. But her condition was not happy. Though her sentence had been revoked, her conviction still stood. Unless some means could be found to reverse it, she was legally a dead woman, with no rights of her own, dependent upon charity. Fortunately Procter's son by an earlier marriage was charitable.

To the scandal of many, the governor accompanied the jail delivery by a general pardon for those accused who had not been tried. Those who had fled from prosecution, like John Alden, and a wealthy Salem merchant named Philip English, were able to come home, and Joseph Putnam to unsaddle the horse he was supposed to be keeping at the ready in his stable. To kinsmen of the accused the pardon was a blessing; to others it was an invitation to disaster. Even Chief Justice Stoughton had once left the bench in his anger at the judges' refusal to convict.

The jail delivery was not, however, universal. None could be released without paying the expense of their keep in prison and the cost of the irons that had been forged for their limbs. There were some whose relatives could not raise the price. A few died in jail for this reason, and for a time it looked as if George Jacobs's granddaughter Margaret would be one of their number.

The terrified girl had at first "confessed," accusing under pressure both her grandfather and George Burroughs. Then her courage revived, and she revoked her confession in time to plead for forgiveness and receive it from both old Jacobs and the unfortunate minister. Only a timely illness had saved her from the gallows. Now there was none to pay her jail fees; her kinsmen were all dead or in flight. The girl would have died in jail had not a compassionate stranger heard of her plight and bought her freedom.

Tituba too was likely to die in jail. That the witchcraft had begun in the parsonage was a heavy charge on the Reverend Samuel Parris. Witch or no, Tituba was somehow in back of the whole trouble, and he never wanted to see her again. But Tituba was released at last, though not to freedom; someone availed himself of the bargain of a likely slave who could be purchased only at the cost of her jail fees. To him Tituba explained her precedent-setting confession; her master had beaten her into it.

Sarah Cloyce still lived; only survivor of Rebecca Nurse's sisters. Her husband bought her freedom, but did not take her to their old home. They moved afield, as far as they could get from the madness of Salem Village and from the uncharity of a pastor who had never once weighed a lifetime of sober carriage and good works against the accusations of a pack of demented girls. Sarah had once slammed the meetinghouse door on Parris. Now she and her husband slammed the door of the village behind them.

If they had remained they could have shared what shortly became a major project on the part of the villagers: the ousting of their pastor.

16

One night long after the trials had ended, Ann's sister Deliverance, with whom she shared a pallet, ran weeping to her parents.

"Annie's sick! Annie's awful sick! The witches have got her."

The parents ran in their nightclothes to the chamber where Ann sat dazed. "Child, what is it?" asked her mother.

The girl wiped the tears from her eyes and stared at her parents as if she hardly knew them. Then her mind cleared.

"It's gone now, Mama. It was nothing."

"She screamed and screamed," said her sister. "I thought the old witch would kill her."

"What witch?" demanded Thomas sharply. Yet he didn't want to know. In these latter shamed days the last thing any Salem Villager wanted to hear about was witchcraft.

"No one," said Ann. "I had a bad dream. It was only a dream."

"What dream?"

"I cannot tell." It was only half a lie. Dreams had a way of fading into nothing when the dreamer woke, but this had not. She still saw a terrible event long buried in her unconscious: the minister Parris coming from his study at the very moment when at her request Tituba was raising the dead. Such a request was not only a sin but a capital crime. Even so, confession would have been possible but for one circumstance; she had been sent on this errand by her mother.

When her parents went back to bed and her sister settled to sleep, Ann lay awake, staring as it were into the dream and its meaning. She now knew what had long been hidden from her; this episode had been the beginning of her affliction, the very root of her old malady. What did it mean? Was it she not those she had accused who was the witch? Was her mother — but from that thought Ann flinched and hid her head under the covers.

But she could not hide from her understanding of the origin of this dream and why it came now. The minister was about to face his congregation with a statement about the witchcraft, a confession some called it. He had lately fallen upon dark days. The revolt within the parish had begun with the sons and sons-in-law of Rebecca Nurse, who refused to attend meeting and to pay their rates. It had spread to those neighbors who at the risk of their lives had testified for Rebecca and had petitioned for John Procter.

They now demanded nothing less than the dismissal

154

of their pastor. Ann's Uncle Joseph had joined them. Thinking of him, another memory burned into Ann's consciousness, his remark about that mysterious woman from the west who had been put to death for trying to raise her child's spirit from the dead. That too was a root of her affliction, a source of her terror and her guilt.

In the dark Ann struggled to control the first symptoms of a convulsion. At last, seeing that her little sister was asleep, she went to the kitchen to spend the rest of the night by the banked ashes of the hearth. She dared not sleep again.

Pale and ill she went with her family to the meeting-house, and waited for the minister to come to the pulpit. What would he say when he got there? Would he report what he had seen when he unexpectedly came from his study? If he did, would she be able to protect her mother, to take the whole guilt upon herself?

Nothing of what she feared took place. The episode so painfully vivid in Ann's mind was not in the minister's at all. What he had happened upon that day so long ago he had not observed. Though he now knew that witchcraft had originated in his parsonage, he connected it not with the visits of the girls but with the episode of the witch cake which John Indian had baked on his hearth to feed to the dog. Of this he indirectly spoke in what he called "A Meditation for Peace."

"I consider it a rare rebuke that the late horrid calamity came first to my own family, that means were used in my house to raise spirits, though totally unknown to me or mine until afterward. I desire to lie

155

low under all this reproach, to lay my hand to my mouth."

The dissenting brethren had accused him of testifying to what he could not know when he reported that witches had struck down the girls in their fits. They accused him of abandoning all charity to accept testimony against the good and the true. Of these matters Parris also spoke. He now admitted that "God may suffer the devil to take the shape of the innocent." He expressed sympathy for "those who had suffered through the clouds of human weakness and Satan's wiles and sophistries." He asked pardon of God and asked that men "from this day forward be covered with the mantle of love and that we forgive each other heartily."

"Had half as much been said before," remarked one of Rebecca's sons, "it would not have come to this."

But Parris's repentance could not amend what he had done. The drive to remove him went on. The General Court of Massachusetts reproved the dissenters; a council of North Shore ministers urged the congregation to forgive its minister now that he was of a better mind. But the dissenters would not rest until they were rid of him.

The address had lightened Ann's fears but not her heart. She too longed to confess and lie low with her hand to her mouth. She had heard a tale from Boston. The entire witch jury had risen in meeting to repent their part in condemning unjustly. The eminent Judge Samuel Sewall had later joined them. Would either judge or jury have condemned without her testimony? There was in her a great longing to repent publicly and ask forgiveness. But the thought of her mother always stopped her. She could not bring shame upon her mother.

It took years for the dissenters to have their way with Parris, and Ann was a young woman grown, already seventeen before they succeeded. Among the Putnams their efforts were seldom discussed; they did not participate, they did not hinder. They looked to the past as seldom as possible, less in guilt than bewilderment. Only when they heard that Mrs. Parris, who was making a feeble recovery from the birth of a son, was sinking into mortal illness, did the elder Ann speak out.

"It is with her as with my poor sister Bayley. They will not let her rest until they kill her."

They? Her daughter shuddered at the word. Was her mother about to hunt witches again? But her mother referred only to the comings and goings at the parsonage of implacable parishioners determined to oust their pastor. She had known that in her dead sister's household, and more — the spying, the spiteful gossip. The burden that had killed her sister was now bearing down on gentle Mrs. Parris. How well she knew it!

"Go to her, Ann," she said. "Go and show our love. Take with you broth and jellies."

Her daughter was dismayed. Not in years had she crossed the parsonage threshold, and she never wanted to see the place again. Could not her mother bring better comfort than she? But she knew she could not, for her mother was again big with child, and the pregnancy was sapping her strength.

157

It had never been in so dutiful a daughter to disobey her mother, and she did not now. Fearfully, she approached the parsonage and found it full of women. The village had rallied as it always did in time of crisis, as it had done during the affliction of the girls. Better then that it had not done so, but who could fault the loving kindness that brought the village women now? Elizabeth Booth's mother rocked the lusty man-child in his cradle. Mary Sibley bent over the hearth to heat a concoction designed to strengthen the frail mother. A murmur of voices came from the chamber where others hovered over the sickbed. Ann thought to leave her little basket and go home when Hannah Ingersoll came from the sickroom.

"Will you see her now?" she asked. "I think she will understand comfortable words from you."

When Ann came, Mrs. Parris fluttered open her eyes. Bending close to the bed, Ann caught a whispered word, "Kind."

"Speak to her, Ann, she'll believe you," said Hannah earnestly. "Tell her this weakness will pass. Tell her that she'll live to see her son in manhood."

Ann could not. It had never been in her to lie. When long ago she had reported what she now knew was false, she had reported truthfully what had been revealed to her under the devil's delusion. She looked into the sunken face, yellow against the white pillow, and knew that Mrs. Parris would never see more of her son than she saw now.

"We go to God for you," she murmured. "My mother and I — you are never absent from our prayers."

The eyes fluttered open again and something like a smile twisted the pale lips. "Kind," whispered Mrs. Parris, and Ann turned to go. Though she was never to know, it was God's mercy that the poor lady did not live to see her babe grow to manhood. For then he fell into a worse affliction than had troubled the girls; he became hopelessly insane.

Mrs. Parris died in 1696, the year when the witch jury made public repentance of its error. A year later Parris finally yielded to pressure, and having managed to collect what was owed him on his "rates," even from the kinsmen of Rebecca Nurse, went his way never to be seen in the village again. For a few months the pulpit was filled by temporary pastors, even for a time by the elder Ann's brother-in-law Bayley. Then the village got a pastor who would stay the course. And it was a new heaven and a new earth, for this was young Joseph Green.

17

The younger Ann had grown into womanhood unspoken for. It was as if her childhood eminence had
created a little space about her which no youth dared
cross. It was not so with other afflicted girls. Between her
fits Mercy Lewis had never wanted for company in the
haymow, not good company perhaps, but company.
Elizabeth Booth and Mercy Walcott, once recovered
from their affliction, had found mates and became re-
spectable matrons. But no one spoke for Ann.

It was not that she lacked comeliness. Blue of eye, fair
of hair, pale, but with the charming pallor of snowdrops, she was not ugly. Her figure, to be sure remained
slight, hardly more developed than in her childhood.
Perhaps it put off youths who craved a buxom armful.

She was approached once, not by the youth himself,
but by a spokesman, her Uncle Joseph. He came to her,
not to her parents, for they were dead. Just before the
turn of the century Thomas Putnam sickened and died,
and his wife, for whom life was inconceivable without

160

him, survived only three months. To Ann was left the sole care of eight brothers and sisters, and to Ann her uncle went.

"My man Francis is too shy to speak for himself. But surely in meeting you have seen how often his eyes turn to you."

Ann had not. In the presence of men she kept her eyes downcast, and in meeting lifted them only to the preacher, young Joseph Green. If she looked to the right or to the left it was only when the restlessness of her siblings required her attention.

"No. Why?" she asked.

"Francis desires your hand in marriage. He has commissioned me to ask for it."

Ann looked at her uncle amazed. Did he think that she, the daughter of Sergeant Putnam, would stoop to become the mate of a landless laborer? As well suggest that she marry William Good, widower of the long dead Sarah, father of the luckless Dorcas. Joseph read her thought.

"He is not to be despised," he said. "Deacon Ingersoll began in no better way, serving for hire until he learned the art of farming and could buy land of his own. I have more acres than I need, and when he leaves my services, I shall deed some to him. With that and your own dower he can face the world. Will you think of it, Ann?"

Ann shook her head. "It is not for me to marry."

"But child, why not?"

"I have my mother's children to raise."

161

The phrase struck her uncle. Were they not also her father's children? Ann had loved and respected her father, but she always referred to her duties in this way. Was it because she had helped her mother bring nearly all her babies into the world, one after another, while her father cowered in the kitchen or sometimes in the stable? Or was it only that first and last Ann was her mother's daughter?

"They are growing fast," said Joseph. "Why should the whole burden be on you? One child helps rear another."

"It is not for me," repeated Ann. "It is not God's will that I marry."

Her uncle read anguish in her eyes and from pity said no more. In meeting that Sabbath Ann once swung her eyes to the opposite side of the house where the hired man Francis sat. From the rigidity with which he fixed his eyes on the pulpit Ann knew that her uncle had given her answer. Did she regret it? Her life was as full as any woman's. She directed the farm, saw the children, the youngest hardly past babyhood, through their illnesses, and taught them. What other occupation could she ask for?

Yet there was an emptiness in her life. In her daily labors she gave little thought to it, but when Sabbath meeting gave her the rare leisure to sit quietly and reflect, it weighed upon her. She lifted her eyes to the young pastor and mutely asked his help.

Joseph Green was as different from Samuel Parris as day from night. He was young, and when he came, a bachelor, though not for long. Once he met Elizabeth Gerrish, daughter of the Wenham minister, it was the end of his bachelorhood. The affection of the young couple was beautiful to see, and in no time the bleak parsonage echoed with the yelpings and cooings of babes.

Green had not long been a pastor, indeed not long a practicing Christian. In his student days at Harvard he had been a sinner who broke the Sabbath by his expeditions to hunt and fish, who scandalized his tutors by his card playing, dancing, and some said his cursing. One would have supposed him headed for damnation, not the ministry.

Grace came to him only after he had taken his degree and went to teach in Roxbury. It came through Cotton Mather, not from personal encounter, but from one of his pamphlets. Which one? Mather loved the printing press almost as much as he loved his own soul, and at the least word of encouragement rushed into print with his latest sermon, and once (most unfortunately for his reputation) with a credulous account of the witchcraft. Whichever publication won the soul of the young teacher, it was not that one. It was a sermon that awoke him to the wickedness of his ways and produced an instant conversion. Overnight he became an evangelist. Until Salem Village called him, he had no settled pulpit, but his preaching as a layman had become famous.

What, doubters asked, could a pastor just turned twenty-two do for the ancient ills of Salem Village? These looked askance at the lively young pastor who relished his mug of ale with the farmhands at Ingersoll's ordinary; attended a house-raising not to look on, but to work with his own hands to help hoist the rooftree, and went to the woods with his fowling piece to shoot wild pigeons (but never on a Sunday). Was this a proper pastor?

But underlying all his gaity was a solemn intent. When he arrived in 1697, two years before the death of Thomas Putnam and his wife, he was determined to bring peace to the strife-torn village. He began at the next "dignifying" of the seats in the meetinghouse by inducing old enemies to sit together. He managed to get Rebecca Nurse's son Samuel to sit by Sergeant Putnam and Rebecca's daughter, the Widow Preston, to share a bench with the elder Ann Putnam.

Socially the arrangement was no success. In meeting the widow Preston and the elder Ann sat eyes forward, averted from each other, and left the meetinghouse without a word of greeting. Through the Widow Preston's mind went the thought, "To lose such a mother in such a way!" The elder Ann thought, in spite of herself, of her dead sister's babies. Were they or were they not murdered by this woman's mother? But neither uttered such thoughts and, stiffly as they sat, their being together was symbolic.

At that time the younger Ann sat apart to care for the youngest Putnams. In her was a great longing to beg pardon of the Widow Preston for what she had done to her mother. But how could she do so without bringing shame on her own?

Ann's parents had been three years in their graves

164

when, in 1702, Green took a bold step. He called on the parish to revoke the excommunication of Martha Cory, and received his first defeat from his parish. Since town meeting, where he made this request, was no place for women, Ann had not attended. Her eldest brother, now technically the head of the family, had done so and came home perplexed.

"Why do they hate her so?" he asked. "She's ten years dead, and some could have been no more spiteful than as if she sat among them. What was there about her?"

"She was one who spoke her mind," said Ann. "And her tongue was sharp."

"And was that all?"

"She asked what is forbidden women, to pray in public."

The shouts of town meeting still echoing in his ears the brother searched his mind for what he in childhood had known of Martha Cory. A memory came.

"Was she after all a witch?" he asked. "I was in the meetinghouse when you saw her take the shape of a yellow bird."

Ann remembered too, unwillingly. "There's no lack of birds in the meetinghouse," she said. "Didn't you see last Sabbath how a little sparrow fluttered about and beat his wings against the shutters?"

"That was a read bird. Martha Cory's was spectral. I looked and looked and saw nothing, but you did, and a child from the parsonage. If she was not a witch how do you explain it?"

Ann did not reply. Her brother's reminiscence had

165

set Martha's yellow bird to fluttering before her inner vision. She swayed with dizziness.

"It's time to get supper," she said.

But her brother could not drop the subject. "I heard a strange thing. I heard that Goody Cory did not believe there were witches. Is it true she said that? Is it possible that with all those hangings there were no witches here after all?"

Ann felt as if a hand had reached to her throat to choke her. "I am unwell," she gasped, and forgetting supper went to her room. She lay there struggling with her old problem. Was it for her to help Parson Green with his peacemaking? If she, like the witch jury and Judge Sewall, made public acknowledgment of her repentance, might Martha Cory be absolved — of a crime she had not committed? She prayed for a sign. Let the minister come to her with such a request and she would obey.

He did not come, she did not speak. A year later he had his way with the parish. Without Ann's help, Martha Cory's name was honorably restored to the church rolls. Thanks to the young minister little Salem Village had done better than the far greater parish in Salem Town. Nine more years were to pass before its congregation could be persuaded to revoke the excommunication of Rebecca Nurse.

It was 1706 before Ann received the sign that sent her to her pastor. It came out of a grave illness. She had never been strong, and the recurrent convulsions of her twelfth year had impaired her health. She recovered

166

slowly from this attack and felt in her bones that another would carry her off.

"Dare I die with a sin unrepented of?" she asked herself, and uttered a strange prayer. "Mother, help me. Mother, is it your will that I confess?"

She heard or thought she heard a voice. "Come to my grave." Ann struggled from her bed, there being no one about to prevent her, and went to the little family graveyard where she had knelt so often with her mother. "Give me a sign," she prayed. "Mother, will you forgive me if to the limit of my understanding I confess?"

There was no outward sign, nor did a vision rise before her as in the old days. She heard no sounds but those of the bees buzzing in the tall hollyhocks and a gentle breeze in the pine boughs overhead. But in the peace of the summer afternoon she felt a blessing.

She questioned no further. Frail as she was she mustered the strength to get into proper dress, saddle the mare, very old now but biddable, and ride the mile through the woods to the parsonage.

"I ask to be received in grace," she told her pastor tremulously. "I ask to lie in the dust and beg forgiveness of God and men for what I did in childhood. Is it possible I can receive it, or are my sins unpardonable?"

"I must question you," said the pastor. Ann shivered. Would he ask her about her mother's part, about that fatal errand to Tituba? But Green had none of the scientific curiosity of Cotton Mather, and no craving to explore the origin of so dark a mystery as the witchcraft. That Ann's mother had played some part he knew, but it was not for him to examine the dead. He wanted only to sound the sincerity of Ann's repentance.

"What was in your heart when you testified?" he asked. "When you cried out on such a one as Rebecca Nurse, was it from malice?"

"I hardly knew her," whispered Ann. She saw a vision now: Rebecca coming into meeting, looking with kind eyes on all about her, one to whom a child could bring her troubles. "Oh, I wish I could have known her!"

"Or Goody Cory. You did not hate her?"

"Her eyes and her tongue were sharp. Some girls hated her for that. She did me no harm."

"Yet you testified . . ."

Ann bowed her head and wept. "I know, I know, and how can it be forgiven me?"

"You lied?"

"It was not a lie but my distraction. I had dreams, I saw visions. The devil had me in the power of his delusion. Perhaps there was no witch there but I. Was I a witch?"

"Did you covenant with the evil one?"

"I did not covenant. I know not how he came or how he had his way with me."

Her strength was running out. The pastor's young wife came into the study and signaled her husband.

"Let her rest, poor woman. You ask more than she can bear."

Later the pastor worked with Ann to compose a confession. He would read it before Sabbath meeting while

168

she stood with bowed head. Then he would ask the congregation its will.

"You know," he said, "it is for the members, not me, to offer you the right hand of fellowship."

"And forgive? Will it be in them to forgive?"

Green did not know. He was in doubt about the Nurse family, who had not rested until they got rid of Parris. He undertook to visit them all before the Sabbath when Ann's confession was to be read, to reason with them and pray. He was not entirely successful. It was August and the high season of work on the farms, and one of Rebecca's sons was always afield when he called. No matter how often Green attempted to track the man down, he was always elsewhere. Nor could he get a firm answer from those he did find.

"Do you know what she did?" asked one. "When our poor mother cried 'Oh God help me!' that child redoubled her howls and accusations. When after the trial the governor in his mercy granted a reprieve, how was it with Ann Putnam? She feigned death until he revoked it."

"Was that not she but another in her household?" asked Green.

"It was she! Do you know that we could bury our mother only in secret? We stole her body at night from the pit where it was thrown. Even now we cannot point out where she lies lest it be accounted a charge against us. If this were your mother, could you forgive?"

"Visit her grave now," urged Green. "Ask your mother what she would have you do."

Ill content with his efforts, he went to Ann and asked her to postpone her confession one more week. "It will give them time for prayer and reflection."

Ann was stricken. "Another week and I may be dead! Must I die with this sin on my soul?"

"That's foolishness, Annie," said her brother. "Another week and you'll be so much stronger."

Ann would not listen. Daily, hourly she had prayed to nerve herself for this ordeal. It must be now or never. Her pastor gave in.

"I desire to be humbled before God." Slowly the minister read Ann's words while she stood in place, eyes downcast, pale as death. "It was a great delusion of Satan that deceived me in that sad time. I did it not out of any anger, malice, or ill will."

The pastor paused to glance at his congregation. Would the Nurse family accept such a statement? He could not easily meet their eyes, for the sons, sons-in-law, daughters and daughters-in-law were widely scattered. He read on.

"And particularly as I was a chief instrument of accusing Goodwife Nurse and her two sisters, I desire to lie in the dust and be humbled for it, in that I was a cause with others of so sad a calamity to them and their families. I desire to lie in the dust and earnestly beg forgiveness of all those unto whom I have given just cause of sorrow and offense, whose relations were taken away and accused."

The reading was over and the critical moment at hand. Would the congregation receive this penitent into fellowship? Green lifted his eyes and put the question to them.

One hand was raised. It was Rebecca's daughter Sarah. Until today she had been in doubt, but that morning she had opened her Bible at random and read, "Father forgive them, for they know not what they do." It was as if her mother had spoken. She raised her hand, and after a pause her brothers, her sisters, and all the congregation followed suit.

Ann collapsed sobbing to her seat, and when the last psalm had been sung, it was Sarah who went to her, placed a strong arm about her shoulders and led her into the sunshine.

Epilogue

Ann, who had feared to die before she could make her confession, lived for some years after. She was not destined "to make old bones," as the country folk put it; in her last years she was often an invalid, but live she did.

There remained that curious little space about her, intensified by her confession, forgiven though she was. In taking the shame and blame of the witchcraft accusations upon herself, she had become a scapegoat, even in her own family. She had no namesakes; for centuries the name Ann Putnam would be avoided among her kin.

Was it so with the other girls who had accused as many as she? Some had left the village: Abigail Williams with her uncle; Mercy Lewis with the migrants to Maine. Some who remained had fallen into ill repute. Two who had married respectably, Mary Walcott and Elizabeth Booth, had lived down the notoriety of their youth. They were present when Ann made her confession. Why did they, guilty as she, let her stand lonely in meeting?

Their affliction was fourteen years in the past; the girls who suffered it might have been strangers, whose motives and behavior were incomprehensible. Why call attention to what was better forgotten, why burden their husbands and children with what was so long past? Newcomers to the village might never hear what they had done under other names. Old-timers all but forgot them in their discussion of the part played by Ann Putnam and her mother.

The younger Ann lived to see many changes brought about by the witchcraft. Two were remote, beyond her knowledge. Old England's laws were in time modified by New England's experience with spectral evidence. English witches were still hanged, but more and more rarely, and never in consequence of a full scale witch-hunt. Nor was it lost on thoughtful observers that once the Salem witch craze gathered momentum, it had been carried on less by the testimony of the girls than that of the "confessors." It eventually became law that a confession not corroborated by other evidence could not be accepted in court as fact.

These things Ann could not know. What she did know was that a few years after she begged pardon in meeting, the Massachusetts General Court undertook to rehabilitate the reputations of many of the condemned and even to make restitution to their families.

A belief that horrible injustice had been done first became manifest in 1696 in the repentance of the witch jury. From that time it gathered strength. It was never universal. There were always some who spoke darkly of "the willful smothering of the witchcraft," and who thought that the condemned were not only guilty but that hanging was too good for them. "They did better in Europe where they burned them at the stake," said these, and the suggestion was to echo centuries later in the ears of visitors to Salem who would affront the local police by asking direction to "the place where the witches were burned."

The actions taken by the General Court of 1710 and 1711 was due primarily to this sense of irreparable wrong, and was in response to the petitions of those who were still handicapped by the past, Elizabeth Procter, free, but still under sentence of death, pleaded for correction of her status so that she could at least claim her dower rights. William Good was calling attention to the deplorable condition of his daughter Dorcas, who had never recovered from the nightmare of prison life.

The first step toward rehabilitation was taken in 1710 when the General Court responded to these petitions by reversing the convictions of several of the condemned, thus pronouncing them guiltless. A year later it made compensation to their families.

This award of compensation was designed to cover the expenses which the survivors had been put to in bringing aid and comfort to their kin. No exorbitant claims were honored. A wealthy Salem man, Philip English, who put in a claim of £1,500 to cover the business losses he had sustained when he fled arrest to New York, did not receive a penny.

Some of the larger amounts may have represented an

attempt to cover what a modern court would call "pain and suffering." Thus the Procter family received £150; the children of George Burroughs, who had bitterly complained that their stepmother had made off with all their father's property, got £50; and the kin of Sarah Good £30. Martha Carrier's family received only £7/6, and oddly enough Abigail Hobbs, who had not been hanged, received £10. Her "confession" had cost the lives of others and her reputation was not good, but Abigail got her award.

The Nurse family refused to put a price on their loss. What mattered most to them was the revocation of their mother's excommunication. The First Church of Salem had taken its time about it. Only in 1712, two years after General Court reversed the attainder against her, did it do so.

Massachusetts had come out of the delusion not without honor. Not every government can be brought to acknowledge a grievous error and attempt to rectify it. Atonement was, however, incomplete. Not all of the condemned had been exonerated, only those who then had survivors to petition for them. The judgments still stood on many, like Bridget Bishop and Ann Pudeator.

Centuries later their descendants, and descendants of others like them, got together to demand that the General Court clear the names of their ancestors. Matters came to a climax in 1954. Massachusetts, long since a sovereign state, was faced with a perplexing problem. Some legislators protested that since the sentences had been imposed when the state was a colony

175

under British rule, action could be properly taken only by the British monarch. One representative said that if the judgments were removed wholesale, their descendants could claim compensation as had been done in 1711. Since descendants had multiplied over the centuries (those of Rebecca Nurse were estimated at thirty thousand), their claims could enormously increase the tax burden of Massachusetts. No one took this objection seriously; an act was passed that pronounced all the condemned guiltless.

Were there no witches at all in Massachusetts in 1692? According to modern law there were none, none at least among the condemned. The ghost of little Ann Putnam, the only accuser who came to her senses and tried to make amends, may still ask, "Was it I? Was I all unwittingly the true witch?"